Study Guide

Macroeconomics for Today

FOURTH EDITION

Irvin B. Tucker

University of North Carolina at Charlotte

R. Moore

THOMSON
™
SOUTH-WESTERN

Australia · Canada · Mexico · Singapore · Spain · United Kingdom · United States

THOMSON

SOUTH-WESTERN

Study Guide for Macroeconomics for Today, 4e

Irvin B. Tucker

VP/Editorial Director:
Jack W. Calhoun

VP/Editor-in-Chief:
Dave Shaut

Publisher and Acquisitions Editor:
Michael B. Mercier

Developmental Editor:
Bob Sandman

Technology Project Editor:
Peggy Buskey

Marketing Manager:
John Carey

Senior Production Editor:
Kara ZumBahlen

Media Editor:
Pam Wallace

Senior Manufacturing Coordinator:
Sandee Milewski

Printer:
West Group, Eagan, MN

Table of Contents

PART IV MONEY, BANKING, AND MONETARY POLICY

PART V THE INTERNATIONAL ECONOMY

PREFACE

How to Use This Study Guide

This *Study Guide* is designed to be used with *Macroeconomics for Today, 4e* and *Alternate Macroeconomics for Today, 4e* by Irvin B. Tucker. The study guide provides drill, repetition, and exercises to identify problems and prepare you for quizzes. Each chapter of the study guide contains several sections. Here are some explanations for each of these sections:

Chapter in a Nutshell and Key Concepts

The Chapter in a Nutshell provides review of the important ideas in the chapter. The Key Concepts section lists the important concepts introduced in the corresponding text chapter. Before proceeding to any of the other sections, you should review each concept by defining it in your mind. If you do not understand any of the concepts, you should reread the appropriate sections in the text chapter.

Master the Learning Objectives

This section lists the key concepts that you will be able to understand after completing each chapter. In addition, "step-by-step" instructions for using Internet instructional features are given on the Tucker Xtra! Web site. Master the Learning Objectives is therefore a unique Internet study guide referenced within the printed version of this study guide.

Economist's Tool Kit

Included in many chapters is a section called "The Economist's Tool Kit." The purpose of this feature is to reach into the economist's collection of basic models and explain each model in a clear step-by-step presentation. You will find this technique a useful supplement to the graphs in the text.

Completion Questions

After you have reviewed the key concepts, you are prepared to work through the completion questions. Each completion question's answer can be found in the Key Concepts section. After filling in the blanks, check yourself by the answers given at the end of the chapter. If you do not know why the answer given is the correct one, refer back to the proper section of the text.

Multiple Choice and True or False Questions

Multiple choice and true or false questions test your understanding of the basic economic concepts presented in the text chapter. Your instructor has a test bank of similar questions from which to choose exam questions. The questions in this study guide provide the types of questions that may be asked. If you have trouble with any of the multiple choice questions or true/false questions, be concerned. Go back to the text and carefully reread the discussion of the concept that is giving you a problem.

Crossword Puzzles

Crossword puzzles provide an interesting way to give you practice in the use of concepts in the chapter.

Additional Learning Resources

Online Quiz

Go to http://tucker.swcollege.com and test your understanding of the chapter's concepts with the interactive quiz. Each quiz contains twenty multiple questions, like those found on a typical exam. Detailed feedback is included for each answer so that you may know instantly why you have answered correctly or incorrectly. In addition, you may email yourself and/or your instructor the quiz results with a listing of correct and incorrect answers. Finally, check your results versus other students around the world—previous scores to quizzes are displayed online.

Practice Quiz PowerPoint Tutorial

This PowerPoint tutorial is perfect for test preparation. This online tutorial is available at the Tucker *Economics for Today* Web Site http://tucker.swlearning.com. First, the end-of-chapter practice questions appear on the screen and then correct answers are explained. Many answers include animated graphs that shift with a click of the mouse, and help students master the graphing process that is so important in understanding the concepts.

Tucker Xtra! Web Site and CD-ROM

Students buying a new textbook packaged with the Tucker Xtra! CD-ROM received complimentary access (via the CD) to the robust set of additional learning tools found at the Tucker Xtra! Web site. If you do not have the CD, you can view a demo and purchase access to the site online at http://tucker.swlearning.com. Here is a tour through some of the powerful study support features that include THE GRAPHING WORKSHOP, a unique learning system made up of tutorials, interactive tools, and exercises that teach students how to interpret, reproduce, and explain graphs; Frequently Asked Questions and CNN video segments; and extensive self-testing opportunities. Students who do not buy a new text/CD package can purchase access to the site online.

The Graphing Workshop

This is a unique learning system included on the Tucker Xtra! CD-ROM described above. For most students, graphing is one of the most difficult aspects of the principles course. THE GRAPHING WORKSHOP is your one-stop learning resource for help in mastering the language of graphs. You'll explore important economic concepts through a unique learning system made up of tutorials, interactive tools, and exercises that teach you how to interpret, reproduce, and explain graphs:

SEE IT! Animated graphing tutorials provide step-by-step graphical presentations and audio explanations.

GRASP IT! Interactive graphing exercises let you practice manipulating and interpreting graphs with a slider bar graphing tool. You can check your work online.

TRY IT! Interactive graphing assignments challenge you to apply what you have learned by creating your own graph from scratch to analyze a specific scenario. You can print out and/or email answers to your instructor for grading.

ANIMATED CAUSATION CHAINS! These games illustrate the cause-and-effect analyis behind the graphs.

Homework Sets

These sets of exercises, prepared by William Weber of Eastern Illinois University, review economic concepts presented in the text. They can be used by students to practice for exams. Answers are found in the Instructor's Manual.

InfoTrac College Edition

If you bought a new copy of the InfoTrac College Edition of this text, don't forget to take advantage of your subscription. With InfoTrac College Edition, you can receive anytime, anywhere, online access to a database of full-text articles from hundreds of scholarly and popular periodicals. You can use its fast and easy search tools to find what you're looking for among the tens of thousands of articles-updated daily and dating back as far as four years-all in this single Web site. It's a great way to locate resources for papers and projects without having to travel to the library. To get started, visit http://www.infotrac-college.com.

The Wall Street Journal Edition

If you bought a new copy of the special Wall Street Journal Edition of the Tucker textbook, a subscription to both the *The Wall Street Journal* Print and Interactive versions was included with your purchase. Be sure to take advantage of all *The Wall Street Journal* has to offer by activating your subscription to this authoritative publication, which is synonymous with the latest word on business, economics, and public policy.

Best of success with your course!

Irvin B. Tucker

CHAPTER CONVERSION TABLE

Macroeconomics for Today	Alternate Macroeconomics for Today
1	1
2	2
3	3
4	4
5	5
5A	5A
6	6
7	7
8	-
9	-
10	8
10A	8A
11	9
12	10
13	11
14	12
15	13
16	14
16A	14A
17	15
18	16
19	17
20	18

Chapter 1
Introducing the Economic Way of Thinking

■ CHAPTER IN A NUTSHELL

The major objective of this chapter is to acquaint the student with the subject of economics. The birth of the Levi Strauss Company introduces the heart of economics: Economics is about people making choices concerning the allocation of scarce resources. This story highlights the success of a young entrepreneur who combined the resources of land, labor, and capital to transform canvas into a new type of pants. Another purpose of this chapter is to introduce the economic way of thinking by explaining steps in the model-building process. Economists use models and theories to focus on critical variables, such as price and quantity consumed, by abstracting from other variables that complicate the analysis. The chapter closes with a discussion of the distinction between positive economics and normative economics, which explains why economists sometimes disagree.

■ KEY CONCEPTS

Capital	Microeconomics
Ceteris paribus	Model
Economics	Normative economics
Entrepreneurship	Positive economics
Labor	Resources
Land	Scarcity
Macroeconomics	

■ MASTER THE LEARNING OBJECTIVES

Please visit the Tucker Xtra! site at http://tuckerxtra.swlearning.com to find the interactive version of the "Master the Learning Objectives" feature.

#1 - Understand that economics is the study of scarcity and decision making.

Step 1   Read the sections in your textbook titled *"The Problem of Scarcity," "Scarce Resources and Production, and "Economics: The Study of Scarcity and Choice."*

Step 2   Read the *EconNews* article titled *"The Price of Work: Breakfast on the Run."* This article describes the problem of scarcity facing professionals.

Step 3   Listen to the *"Ask the Instructor Video Clip"* titled *"Why Is Economics Difficult for a lot of Students?"* You will learn that economics relates to the real world using graphs and the jargon of economics.

Step 4   Listen to the *"Ask the Instructor Video Clip"* titled *"What is Macroeconomics?"* You will learn topics studies under macroeconomics.

The Result   Following these steps, you have learned that scarcity forces people to make economic choices, and you will be able to define resources including, land, labor, and capital. You have also learned that microeconomics examines individual markets, and macroeconomics takes an aggregate view of the whole economy.

#2 - Know how economists use a model to explain the relationship between variables, and understand pitfalls of economic reasoning.

Step 1   Read the section in your textbook titled *"The Methodology of Economics," "Hazards of the Economic Way of Thinking"* and *"Why Do Economists Disagree?"*

Step 2   Play the *"Causation Chains Game"* titled *"The Steps in the Model-Building Process."*

Step 3   Listen to the *"Ask the Instructor Video Clip"* titled *"Why Do Economists talk about Money and Wealth? Do They Really Believe that People Are Motivated only by Money?"* You will learn that economists use only models with measurable data.

Step 4   Listen to the *"Ask the Instructor Video Clip"* titled *"Have Computers Affected Worker Productivity?"* You will learn the difference between association and causation.

The Result   Following the steps, you have learned that economists use models to reach conclusions that can be measured by abstracting from reality and holding other factors constant. You have also learned that failing to hold other factors constant (*ceteris paribus* assumption) or confusing association and causation results in flawed economic reasoning. You also know that positive economics is based on testable statements and normative economics is based on opinions.

■ COMPLETION QUESTIONS

1. _____ is the fundamental economic problem that human wants exceed the availability of time, goods, and resources.

2. _____ is the study of how individuals and society choose to allocate scarce resources to satisfy unlimited wants.

3. Factors of production classified as: land, labor, and capital are also called _____.

4. _____ applies an economywide perspective which focuses on such issues as inflation, unemployment, and the growth rate of the economy.

5. _____ examines small units of an economy, analyzing individual markets such as the market for personal computers.

6. A simplified description of reality used to understand and predict economic events is called a (an) _____.

7. If the _____ assumption is violated, a model cannot be tested.

8. _____ uses testable statements.

9. _____ is a shorthand expression for any natural resource provided by nature.

10. The physical plants, machinery, and equipment used to produce other goods. Capital goods are man-made goods that do not directly satisfy human wants is _____.

11. The mental and physical capacity of workers to produce goods and services is _____.

12. _____ is the creative ability of individuals to seek profits by combining resources to produce innovative products.

13. _____ is an analysis based on value judgment.

■ MULTIPLE CHOICE

1.   The condition of scarcity:

   a.   cannot be eliminated.
   b.   prevails in poor economies.
   c.   prevails in rich economies.
   d.   All of the above are true.

2.   The condition of scarcity can be eliminated if:

   a.   people satisfy needs rather than false wants.
   b.   sufficient new resources were discovered.
   c.   output of goods and services were increased.
   d.   none of the above are true.

3.   Which of the following is *not* a factor of production?

   a.   A computer chip.
   b.   The service of a lawyer.
   c.   Dollars.
   d.   All of the above are factors of production.
   e.   None of the above.

4.   A textbook is an example of:

   a.   capital.
   b.   a natural resource.
   c.   labor.
   d.   none of the above.

5.   The subject of economics is primarily the study of:

   a.   the government decision-making process.
   b.   how to operate a business successfully.
   c.   decision-making because of the problem of scarcity.
   d.   how to make money in the stock market.

6.   Which of the following is included in the study of macroeconomics?

   a.   Salaries of college professors.
   b.   Computer prices.
   c.   Unemployment in the nation.
   d.   Silver prices.

7.   Microeconomics approaches the study of economics from the viewpoint of:

   a.   individual or specific markets.
   b.   the national economy.
   c.   government units.
   d.   economywide markets.

8.   The definition of a model is a:

   a.   description of all variables affecting a situation.
   b.   positive analysis of all variables affecting an event.
   c.   simplified description of reality to understand and predict an economic event.
   d.   data adjusted for rational action.

9.   Which of the following is a positive statement?

   a.   I think we should pass a constitutional amendment to reduce the deficit.
   b.   President Clinton's way of dealing with the economy is better than President Bush's.
   c.   I hope interest rates come down soon.
   d.   If taxes are raised, unemployment will drop.

10.   "An increase in the federal minimum wage will provide a living wage for the working poor" is a:

   a.   statement of positive economics.
   b.   fallacy of composition.
   c.   tautology.
   d.   statement of normative economics.

11.   Select the normative statement that completes the following sentence: If the minimum wage is raised:

   a.   cost per unit of output will rise.
   b.   workers will gain their rightful share of total income.
   c.   the rate of inflation will increase.
   d.   profits will fall.

12.   "The government should provide health care for all citizens." This statement is an illustration of:

a.   positive economic analysis.
b.   correlation analysis.
c.   fallacy of association analysis.
d.   normative economic analysis.

13.   The software programs that make computer hardware useful in production and management tasks are:

a.   capital.
b.   labor.
c.   a natural resource.
d.   None of the above.

14.   An economic theory claims that a rise in gasoline prices will cause gasoline purchases to fall, ceteris paribus. The phrase "ceteris paribus" means that:

a.   other relevant factors like consumer incomes must be held constant.
b.   the gasoline prices must first be adjusted for inflation.
c.   the theory is widely accepted but cannot be accurately tested.
d.   consumers' need for gasoline remains the same regardless of the price.

15.   "The federal minimum wage causes higher unemployment among teenagers" is a:

a.   statement of positive economics.
b.   statement of normative economics.
c.   testable value judgment.
d.   fallacy of composition.

16.   Which of the following would eliminate scarcity as an economic problem?

a.   Moderation of people's competitive instincts.
b.   Discovery of sufficiently large new energy reserves.
c.   Resumption of steady productivity growth.
d.   None of the above.

17.   All of the following are examples of capital *except:*

    a.   the robot used to help produce your car.
    b.   a computer used by your professor to write this exam.
    c.   the factory that produces the costume jewelry you buy.
    d.   the inventory of unsold goods at your local hardware store.
    e.   an uncut diamond that you discover in your backyard.

18.   Which of the following would *not* be classified as a capital resource?

    a.   The Empire State Building.
    b.   A Caterpillar bulldozer.
    c.   A Macintosh computer.
    d.   100 shares of stock in General Motors.

19.   If a textbook price rises and then students reduce the quantity demanded of textbooks, an economic model can show a cause-and-effect relationship only if which of the following occurs?

    a.   students' incomes fall.
    b.   tuition decreases.
    c.   the number of students increases.
    d.   all other factors are held constant.
    e.   the bookstore no longer accepts used book trade-ins.

■ TRUE OR FALSE

1.   T   F   All human wants cannot be satisfied because of the problem of scarcity.

2.   T   F   Economics is the study of people's making choices faced with the problem of unlimited wants and limited resources.

3.   T   F   Policies to determine the price of troll dolls are a concern of macroeconomics.

4.   T   F   Policies to increase the supply of money in the economy are primarily a concern of microeconomics.

5.   T   F   The statement "A tax hike for the rich is the fairest way to raise tax collections" is an example of positive economic analysis.

6.   T   F   The statement "The income tax is unfair to those who work hard to earn their incomes" is an example of positive economic analysis.

7.   T   F   The statement "It would be better to put up with price controls than to have continuing higher medical care prices" is an example of normative economic analysis.

8.   T   F   The statement "Cutting government spending is the best way to boost consumer confidence" is an example of normative economics.

9.   T   F   The statement "It is better to suffer a little more unemployment and a little lower prices" is an example of normative economic analysis.

10.   T   F   The statement "American workers are lazy" is an example of positive economic analysis.

■ CROSSWORD PUZZLE

Fill in the crossword puzzle from the list of key concepts. Not all of the concepts are used.

ACROSS

2.   An individual that seeks profits by combining resources to produce innovative products.
4.   The basic categories of inputs used to produce goods and services.
7.   The mental and physical capacity of workers to produce.
8.   A natural resource.
9.   Man-made goods used to produce other goods.
10.   _____ economics is an analysis limited to statements that are verifable by reference to facts.

DOWN

1.   A phrase that means that while certain variables change, "all other things remain unchanged or constant."
2.   The study of how society chooses to allocate its scarce resources to satisfy unlimited wants.
3.   _____ economics is an analysis based on value judgement which cannot be proven by facts.
5.   The condition that human wants are forever greater than supply.
6.   A simplified description of reality.

■ ANSWERS

Completion Questions

1. scarcity
2. economics
3. resources
4. macroeconomics
5. microeconomics
6. model
7. ceteris paribus
8. positive economics
9. land
10. capital
11. labor
12. entrepreneurship
13. normative economics

Multiple Choice

1. d 2. d 3. c 4. a 5. c 6. c 7. a 8. c 9. d 10. d 11. b 12. d 13. a 14. a 15. a 16. d 17. e 18. d 19. d

True or False

1. True 2. True 3. False 4. False 5. False 6. False 7. True 8. True 9. True 10. False

Crossword Puzzle

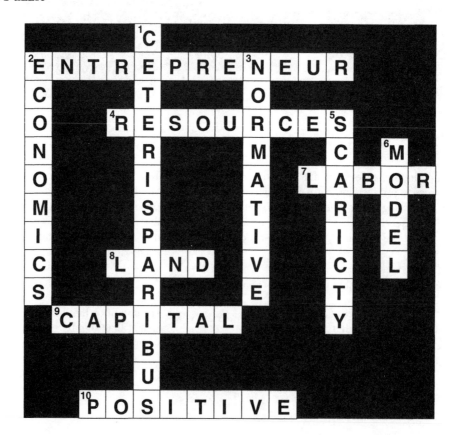

Chapter 1A
Applying Graphs to Economics

■ CHAPTER IN A NUTSHELL

In economics, information is best and most easily displayed by variables in a graph. If one variable rises as the other rises, the two variables are directly related. If one variable rises as the other falls, the two variables are inversely related. The slope of a line is the ratio of the change in the variable on the vertical axis to the change in the variable on the horizontal axis. An upward-sloping line represents two variables that are directly related. A downward-sloping line represents two variables that are inversely related. If one variable rises, as the other remains constant, or unchanged, the two variables are independent. Economists also use three-variable, multi-curve graphs. Using this approach, the relationship between the variables on the X and Y axis, such as price and quantity demanded, are represented by separate lines. The location of each individual line on the graph is determined by a third variable such as annual income.

■ KEY CONCEPTS

> Direct relationship
> Independent relationship
> Inverse relationship
> Slope

■ MASTER THE LEARNING OBJECTIVES

Please visit the Tucker Xtra! site at http://tuckerxtra.swlearning.com to find the interactive version of the "Master the Learning Objectives" feature.

#1 - Use a graph to plot a direct (positive) or an inverse (negative) relationship, and measure the slope of a straight line or curve.

Step 1	Read the sections in your textbook titled *"A Direct Relationship," "An Inverse Relationship," "The Slope of a Straight Line,"* and *"The Slope of a Curve."*
Step 2	Watch the Graphing Workshop *"See It!"* tutorial titled *"Interpreting Graphs."* Study how changes in one variable are related to changes in another variable.
Step 3	Watch the Graphing Workshop *"See It!"* tutorial titled *"Interpreting Graphs."* Study how slopes are computed.
Step 4	Create a new graph a the Graphing Workshop *"Try It!"* exercise titled *"Working with Graphs."* This exercise illustrates the downward-sloping and upward-sloping portion of a curve.

The Result   Following these steps, you have learned to interpret direct (positive) and inverse (negative) relationships using economic variables on the X and Y axes of a graph. You have also learned how to compute the positive or negative slope of a straight line or a curve.

#2 - Understand how economists use a multi-curve graph to represent a three-variable relationship in a two-dimensional graph.

Step 1   Read the sections in your textbook titled *"A Three-Variable Relationship in One Graph"* and *"A Helpful Study Hint Using Graphs."*

Step 2   Read the Graphing Workshop *"Grasp It!"* exercise titled *"Working with Graphs."* This exercise uses a slider bar to demonstrate shifts in a supply curve because of a change in the cost of producing a product.

The Result   Following these steps, you have learned how changes in factors not shown in a graph shift the curve or straight line drawn in the graph.

■ COMPLETION QUESTIONS

1.   A _____ provides a means to clearly show economic relationships in a two-dimensional space.

2.   A (an) _____ is one in which two variables change in the same direction.

3.   A (an) _____ is one in which two variables change in the opposite direction.

4.   The ratio of the vertical change (the rise or fall) to the horizontal change (the run) is called the _____.

5.   A (an) _____ is one in which two variables are unrelated .

■ MULTIPLE CHOICE

Exhibit 1 Straight line

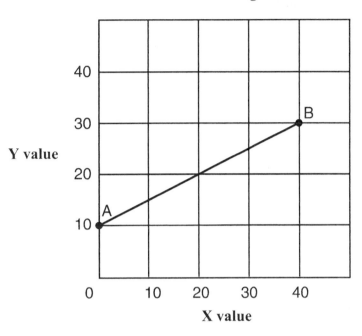

1.   Straight line AB in Exhibit 1 shows that:

    a.   increasing values for X will decrease the values of Y.
    b.   decreasing values for X will increase the values of Y.
    c.   there is a direct relationship between X and Y.
    d.   all of the above.
    e.   none of the above.

2.   In Exhibit 1, the slope of straight line AB is:

    a.   positive.
    b.   zero.
    c.   negative.
    d.   variable.

3.   In Exhibit 1, the slope of straight line AB is:

    a.   1.
    b.   5.
    c.   1/2.
    d.   -1.

4.   As shown in Exhibit 1, the slope of straight line AB:

    a.   decreases with increases in X.
    b.   increases with increases in X.
    c.   increases with decreases in X.
    d.   remains constant with changes in X.

5.   In Exhibit 1, as X increases along the horizontal axis, corresponding to points A-B on the line, the Y values increase. The relationship between the X and Y variables is:

    a.   direct.
    b.   inverse.
    c.   independent.
    d.   variable.

Exhibit 2 Straight line

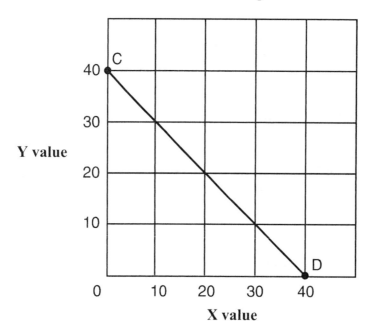

6.   Straight line CD in Exhibit 2 shows that:

    a.   increasing values for X increases the value of Y.
    b.   decreasing values for X decreases the value of Y.
    c.   there is an inverse relationship between X and Y.
    d.   all of the above.
    e.   none of the above.

7.   In Exhibit 2, the slope of straight line CD is:

    a.   positive.
    b.   zero.
    c.   negative.
    d.   variable.

8.   In Exhibit 2, the slope for straight line CD is:

    a.   5.
    b.   1.
    c.   -1.
    d.   -5.

9.   As shown in Exhibit 2, the slope of straight line CD:

    a.   decreases with increases in X.
    b.   increases with increases in X.
    c.   increases with decreases in X.
    d.   remains constant with changes in X.

10.   In Exhibit 2, as X increases along the horizontal axis, corresponding to points C-D on the line, the Y values decrease. The relationship between the X and Y variables is:

    a.   direct.
    b.   inverse.
    c.   independent.
    d.   variable.

Exhibit 3 Straight line

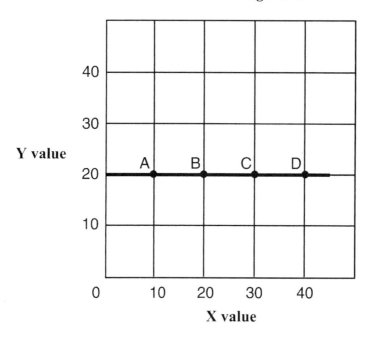

11.   Straight line A-D in Exhibit 3 shows that:

a.   increasing value for X will increase the value of Y.
b.   increasing value for X will decrease the value of Y.
c.   increasing values for X do not affect the value of Y.
d.   all of the above.
e.   none of the above.

12.   In Exhibit 3, the slope of straight line A-D is:

a.   positive.
b.   zero.
c.   negative.
d.   variable.

13.   In Exhibit 3, the slope of the straight line A-D is:

a.   0.
b.   1.
c.   1/2.
d.   -1.

14.   In Exhibit 3, as X increases along the horizontal axis, corresponding to points A-D on the line, the Y values remain unchanged at 20 units. The relationship between the X and Y variables is:

a.   direct.
b.   inverse.
c.   independent.
d.   undefined.

Exhibit 4 Multi-curve graph

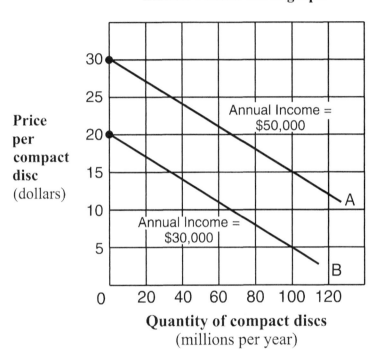

15.   Exhibit 4 represents a three-variable relationship. As the annual income of consumers falls from $50,000 (line A) to $30,000 (line B), the result is a (an):

a.   upward movement along each curve.
b.   downward movement along each curve.
c.   leftward shift in curve A.
d.   rightward shift in curve B.

16.   Measured between two points on a curve, the ratio of the change in the variable on the vertical axis to the change in the variable on the horizontal axis is the:

    a.   axis.
    b.   slope.
    c.   dependent curve.
    d.   independent curve.

17.   A line that has a different slope at each point is s:

    a.   curve.
    b.   straight line.
    c.   vertical line.
    d.   horizontal line.

18.   In a graphic relationship, shifts in a curve are caused by a change in:

    a.   the slope of the curve.
    b.   a factor not measured on the axes of the graph.
    c.   one of the factors measured on either axes of the graph.
    d.   any factor, whether measured on the axes of the graph or not.

19.   A change in a third variable *not* on either axis of a graph is illustrated with:

    a.   a horizontal or vertical line.
    b.   a movement along a curve.
    c.   a shift of a curve.
    d.   a point of intersection.

■ ANSWERS

Completion Questions

1. graph
2. direct relationship
3. inverse relationship
4. slope
5. independent relationship

Multiple Choice

1. c 2. a 3. c 4. d 5. a 6. c 7. c 8. c 9. d 10. b 11. c 12. b 13. a 14. c 15. c 16. b 17. a 18. b
19. c

Chapter 2
Production Possibilities, Opportunity Cost, and Economic Growth

■ CHAPTER IN A NUTSHELL

In this chapter, you continue your quest to learn the economic way of thinking. The chapter begins with the three basic questions each economy must answer: (1) What to produce? (2) How to produce? and (3) For whom to produce? The chapter then introduces concepts which economists use to analyze choice-the production possibilities curve and opportunity costs. The production possibilities curve indicates various maximum combinations of the output of two goods a simple economy can produce. The economy can achieve economic growth by pushing the production possibilities curve outward. This shift in the curve can be caused by increasing resources and/or advances in technology.

■ KEY CONCEPTS

Economic growth	Opportunity cost
Investment	Production possibilities curve
Law of increasing opportunity costs	Technology
Marginal analysis	What, How, and For Whom questions

■ MASTER THE LEARNING OBJECTIVES

Please visit the Tucker Xtra! site at http://tuckerxtra.swlearning.com to find the interactive version of the "Master the Learning Objectives" feature.

#1 - Define the three fundamental economic questions and opportunity cost.

Step 1   Read the sections in your textbook titled *"The Three Fundamental Economic Questions"* and *"Opportunity Cost."*

Step 2   Listen to the *"Ask the Instructor Video Clip"* titled *"Why Do Language Teachers Earn Less?"* You will learn that opportunity cost applies to earnings differentials.

Step 3   Read the *EconNews* article titled *"It's Getting Too Expensive to Put People in Jail."* This article describes the opportunity cost of fighting crime.

Step 4   Read the *EconDebate* titled *"Does Public Investment in Municipal Stadiums Pay Off?"* This article describes how stadiums result in opportunity costs.

The Result   After following these steps, you have learned to understand that all nations must answer three basic economic questions and give examples of opportunity cost.

#2 - Graphically express a production possibilities model and understand that it illustrates marginal analysis, opportunity cost, production efficiency, and inefficiency.

Step 1   Read the sections in your textbook titled *"Marginal Analysis," "The Production Possibilities Curve,"* and *"The Law of Increasing Opportunity Costs."*

Step 2   Watch the Graphing Workshop *"See It!"* tutorial titled *"The Production Possibility."* Study how the production possibilities curve is applied to health care using marginal analysis and the law of increasing opportunity cost. Efficient and inefficient points are also explained in this exercise.

Step 3   Listen to the *"Ask the Instructor Video Clip"* titled *"Why Do Economists Emphasize Marginal Analysis?"* You will learn that marginal analysis is important in career decisions or driving a car.

Step 4   Read the *EconNews* article titled *"The Federal Budget: What a Difference a Day Makes."* This article describes a production possibilities are relationship between national defense and domestic programs.

The Result   After following these steps, you have learned to define marginal analysis and apply this reasoning tool to the production possibilities curve model.

#3 - Use the production possibilities curve to understand economic growth.

Step 1   Read the sections in your textbook titled *"Source of Economic Growth"* and *"Present Investment and the Future Production Possibilities Curve."*

Step 2   Read the Graphing Workshop *"Grasp It!"* exercise titled *"Production Possibilities."* This exercise uses a slider bar to demonstrate economic growth based on the impact of technological change on the production possibilities curve for computers and cars.

Step 3   Create a new graph at the Graphing Workshop *"Try It!"* exercise titled *"Production Possibilities."* This exercise illustrates an outward shift in the production possibilities curve.

Step 4   Play the *"Causation Chains Game"* titled *"Economic Growth and Technology."*

Step 5   Listen to the *"Ask the Instructor Video Clip"* titled *"Do Economists and the General Public Attach Different Meanings to the Term Investment?"* You will learn the economist's definition of investment versus the everyday use of this term.

Step 6   Read the *Econ Debate* article titled *"Is There a New Economy?"* This article describes the issues and background for the "new economy."

The Result   After following these steps, you have learned to explain economic growth in terms of an outward shift in the production possibilities curve.

THE ECONOMIST'S TOOL KIT
Plotting the Production Possibilities Curve

Step one: Draw and label a set of coordinate axes.

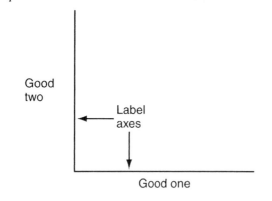

Step two: Plot the maximum quantity that can be produced if all resources are used to produce only good one.

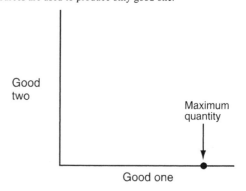

Step three: Plot the maximum quantity that can be produced if all resources are used to produce only good two.

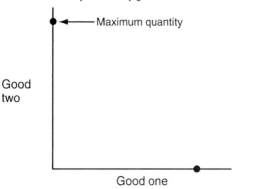

Step four: Plot other maximum possible combinations of both goods that can be produced if all resources are used to produce only two goods.

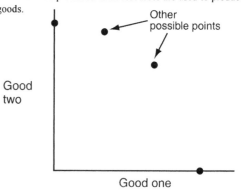

Step five: Draw a smooth curve connecting these points and label it PPC. This curve is the production possibilities curve.

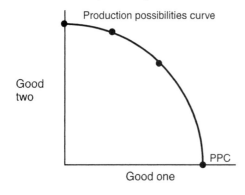

Step six: Verify that increasing opportunity, measured on the vertical axis, occurs as equal increments of good one are produced along the horizontal axis and the slope gets steeper.

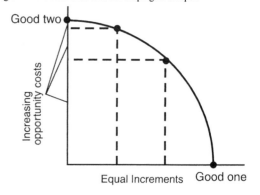

■ COMPLETION QUESTIONS

1. The _____ problem concerns the division of output among society's citizens. The _____ question asks exactly which goods are to be produced and in what quantities. The _____ question requires society to decide the resource mix used to produce goods.

2. _____ is the best alternative forgone for a chosen option.

3. The basic approach that compares additional benefits of a change against the additional costs of the change is called _____.

4. The _____ represents the maximum possible combinations of two outputs that can be produced in a given period of time. Inefficient production occurs at any point inside the curve and all points along the curve are efficient points.

5. The _____ states that the opportunity cost increases as production of an output expands.

6. _____ occurs when the production possibilities curve shifts outward as the result of changes in the resource base or advance in technology.

7. Factories, equipment, and inventories produced in the present are called _____which can be used to shift the production possibilities curve outward in the future.

8. The body of knowledge and skills applied to how goods are produced is _____.

■ MULTIPLE CHOICE

1. Which of the following does *not* illustrate opportunity cost?

    a. If I study, I must give up going to the football game.
    b. If I buy a computer, I must do without a 35" television.
    c. *More* consumer spending now means *more* spending in the future.
    d. If I spend more on clothes, I must spend less on food.

2.   Which of the following would be *most* likely to cause the production possibility curve for computers and education to shift outward?

    a.   A choice of more computers and less education.
    b.   A choice of more education and less computers.
    c.   A reduction in the labor force.
    d.   An increase in the quantity of resources.

Exhibit 1 Production possibility curve data

	A	B	C	D	E	F
Capital goods	15	14	12	9	5	0
Consumer goods	0	2	4	6	8	10

3.   As shown in Exhibit 1, the concept of increasing opportunity costs is reflected in the fact that:

    a.   the quantity of consumer goods produced can never be zero.
    b.   the labor force in the economy is homogeneous.
    c.   greater amounts of capital goods must be sacrificed to produce an additional 2 units of consumer goods.
    d.   a graph of the production data is a downward-sloping straight line.

4.   As shown in Exhibit 1, a total output of 0 units of capital goods and 10 units of consumer goods is:

    a.   the maximum possible output of capital goods for this economy.
    b.   an inefficient way of using the economy's scarce resources.
    c.   the result of efficient use of the economy's resources.
    d.   unobtainable in this economy.

5.   As shown in Exhibit 1, a total output of 14 units of capital goods and 0 units of consumer goods is:

    a.   the result of maximum use of the economy's labor force.
    b.   an efficient way of using the economy's scarce resources.
    c.   unobtainable in this economy.
    d.   less than the maximum rate of output for this economy.

Exhibit 2 Production possibilities curve

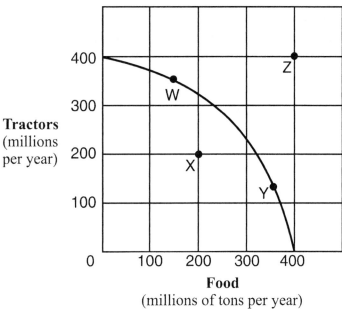

6.   If the economy represented in Exhibit 2 is operating at Point W:

a.   no tractor production must be forgone to produce more food in the current period.
b.   resources are not fully used.
c.   some tractor production must be forgone to produce more food in the current period.
d.   increased food production would be impossible.

7.   Which of the following moves from one point to another in Exhibit 2 would represent an increase in economic efficiency?

a.   Z to W.
b.   W to Y.
c.   W to X.
d.   X to Y.

8.   Movement along this production possibilities curve shown in Exhibit 2 indicates:

a.   that labor is not equally productive or homogeneous.
b.   declining opportunity costs.
c.   all inputs are homogeneous.
d.   all of the above.

9.   In order for the economy shown in Exhibit 2 to reach point Z, it must:

    a.   suffer resource unemployment.
    b.   experience an increase in its resources and/or an improvement in its technology.
    c.   use its resources more efficiently than at point W or Y.
    d.   all of the above.

10.   The following two alternatives exist for a student who has one evening in which to prepare for two exams on the following day:

Possibility	Score in Economics	Score in Accounting
A	95	80
B	80	90

The opportunity cost of receiving a 90 rather than an 80 on the accounting exam is represented by how many points on the economics exam?

    a.   15 points.
    b.   80 points.
    c.   90 points.
    d.   10 points.

11.   On a production possibilities curve, a change from economic inefficiency to economic efficiency is obtained by:

    a.   movement along the curve.
    b.   movement from outside the frontier to a point on the curve.
    c.   movement from a point inside the frontier to a point on the curve.
    d.   a change in the slope of the curve.

12.   One of the assumptions underlying the production possibilities curve for any given economy is that:

    a.   the state of technology is changing.
    b.   there is an unlimited supply of available resources.
    c.   there is full employment and no underemployment of resources when the economy is operating on the curve.
    d.   goods can be produced in unlimited quantities.

13.   Any point on the production possibilities curve illustrates:

    a.   minimum production combinations.
    b.   maximum production combinations.
    c.   economic growth.
    d.   a nonfeasible production combination.

14.   A production possibilities curve has "good X" on the horizontal axis and "good Y" on the vertical axis. On this diagram, the opportunity cost of good X, in terms of good Y, is represented by the:

    a.   distance to the curve from the horizontal axis.
    b.   distance to curve from the vertical axis.
    c.   movement along the curve.
    d.   none of the above.

15.   As production of a good increases, opportunity costs rise because:

    a.   there will be more inefficiency.
    b.   people always prefer having more goods.
    c.   of inflationary pressures.
    d.   workers are not equally suited to all tasks.

16.   Which of the following would be *most* likely to cause the production possibility curve for tanks and cars to shift outward?

    a.   A reduction in the labor force.
    b.   A choice of more tanks and fewer cars.
    c.   A choice of more cars and fewer tanks.
    d.   An increase in the quantity of natural resources.

■ TRUE OR FALSE

1.   T   F   The opportunity cost of a good is the good or service forgone for a chosen good or service.

2.   T   F   If some resources were used inefficiently, the economy would tend to operate outside its production possibilities curve.

3.   T   F   Of all the points on the production possibilities curve, only one point represents an efficient division of labor.

4.   T   F   The most efficient point on the production possibilities curve is the midpoint on the curve.

5.   T   F   On the production possibilities curve, a movement between points that yields a loss of one good in order to raise the output of another good will maintain efficient production.

6.   T   F   If more of one good can be produced without loss of output of another along the same production possibilities curve, the economy must have been operating efficiently.

7.   T   F   All points on the production possibilities curve represent efficient levels of production.

8.   T   F   Investment is an economic term for the act of increasing the stock of money available for business loans.

■ CROSSWORD PUZZLE

Fill in the crossword puzzle from the list of key concepts. Not all of the concepts are used.

ACROSS

2. The accumulation of capital.
7. The basic economic question of which resources to use in production.
8. The basic economic question of which goods and services to produce.
9. The best alternative sacrificed.

DOWN

1. The application of knowledge to production.
3. An outward shift of the production possibilities curve.
4. The ____ possibilities curve shows the maximum combinations of two outputs than an economy can produce, given its available resources and technology.
5. The basic economic question of who receives goods and services.
6. _____ analysis means additions to or subtractions from a current situation.

■ ANSWERS

Completion Questions

1. for whom, what, how
2. opportunity cost
3. marginal analysis
4. production possibilities curve
5. law of increasing opportunity costs
6. economic growth
7. investment
8. technology

Multiple Choice

1. c 2. d 3. c 4. c 5. d 6. c 7. d 8. a 9. b 10. a 11. c 12. c 13. b 14. c 15. d 16. d

True or False

1. True 2. False 3. False 4. False 5. True 6. False 7. True 8. False

Crossword Puzzle

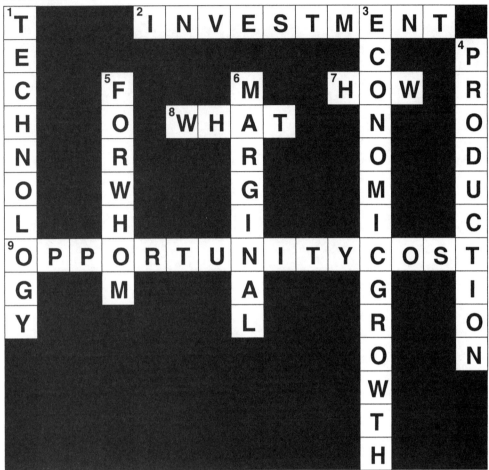

Chapter 3
Market Demand and Supply

■ CHAPTER IN A NUTSHELL

Understanding the price system is a crucial milestone on your quest to learn the economic way of thinking and analyze real-world economic issues. There are two sides to a market: the market demand curve and the market supply curve. The location of the demand curve shifts when changes occur in such nonprice factors as: the number of buyers, tastes and preferences, income, expectations, and the prices of related goods. The location of the supply curve shifts when changes occur in such nonprice factors as: the number of sellers, technology, resource prices, taxes and subsidies, expectations, and prices of other goods. Ceteris paribus, the intersection of the market demand and supply curves determines the equilibrium price and equilibrium quantity of goods.

■ KEY CONCEPTS

Change in demand   Equilibrium   Price system
Change in quantity demanded   Inferior good   Shortage
Change in quantity supplied   Law of demand   Substitute good
Change in supply   Law of supply   Supply
Complementary good   Market   Surplus
Demand   Normal good

■ MASTER THE LEARNING OBJECTIVES

Please visit the Tucker Xtra! site at http://tuckerxtra.swlearning.com to find the interactive version of the "Master the Learning Objectives" feature.

#1 - Understand that a "change in quantity demanded" is a movement along a demand curve, and a "change in demand" is a shift in the demand curve.

Step 1   Read the sections in your textbook titled *"Law of Demand," "The Distinction Between Changes in Quantity Demanded and Change in Demand"* and *"Nonprice Determinants of Demand."*

Step 2   Watch the Graphing Workshop *"See It!"* tutorial titled *"Demand, Shifts in Demand."* Study the factors that shift the demand for milk.

Step 3   Read the Graphing Workshop *"Grasp It!"* exercise titled *"Demand."* This exercise uses a slider bar to demonstrate the concept of demand using the daily demand for hamburgers in a medium-sized city.

Step 4   Create a new graph at the Graphing Workshop *"Try It!"* exercise titled *"Demand."* This exercise illustrates the impact of a change in income on the demand for CDs.

Step 5   Play the *"Causation Chains Game"* titled *"Movement Along a Demand Curve Versus a Shift in Demand."*

Step 6   Listen to the *"Ask the Instructor Video Clip"* titled *"What Factors Affect the Auction Price of Your House?"* Notice the nonprice determinants of demand that affect the price of a house at an auction.

Step 7   Listen to the *"Ask the Instructor Video Clip"* titled *"How Would You Like to be in the "Inferior" Goods Business?"* You will learn the economist's definition of inferior goods versus the everyday use of this term.

Step 8   Watch the *CNN Video Clip* titled *"Smokers and the Bandit"* and analyze how smoking behavior responded to a price hike.

Step 9   Read the *EconNews* article titled *"I'll Replace that Hip for $49.95."* This article describes how lower prices increased the quantity of health care in India.

The Result By following the steps above, you have learned that demand describes buyer behavior and a change in the price for a good or service causes a movement along a demand curve. You have also learned that changes in nonprice factors shift the demand curve leftward or rightward.

#2 - Understand that a "change in quantity supplied" is a movement along a supply curve, and a "change in supply" is a shift in the supply curve.

Step 1   Read the sections in your textbook titled *"Law of Supply," "The Distinction Between Changes in Quantity Supplied and Change in Supply"* and *"Nonprice Determinants of Supply."*

Step 2   Watch the Graphing Workshop *"See It!"* tutorial titled *"Supply, Shifts in Supply."* Study the factors that shift the supply for milk.

Step 3   Read the Graphing Workshop *"Grasp It!"* exercise titled *"Supply."* This exercise uses a slider bar to demonstrate the concept of supply using the daily supply of hamburgers in a medium-sized city.

Step 4   Create a new graph at the Graphing Workshop *"Try It!"* exercise titled *"Supply."* This exercise illustrates the impact of a change in income on the supply of personal computers.

Step 5   Play the *"Causation Chains Game"* titled *"Movement Along a Supply Curve Versus a Shift in Supply."*

Step 6   Read the *EconNews* article titled *"Airlines Are in for a Long Road This Summer."* This article describes how cost increases have shifted the supply curve in the airline industry.

The Result   By following the steps above, you have learned that supply describes seller behavior and a change in the price for a good or service causes a movement along the supply curve. You have also learned changes in nonprice factors shift the supply curve leftward or rightward.

#3 - Understand that equilibrium exists at the price and quantity where the quantity demanded equals the quantity supplied.

Step 1   Read the section in your textbook titled *"A Market Supply and Demand Analysis."*

Step 2   Watch the Graphing Workshop *"See It!"* tutorial titled *"Market Equilibrium."* Study how market equilibrium is established for milk.

Step 3   Read the Graphing Workshop *"Grasp It!"* exercise titled *"Market Equilibrium."* This exercise uses a slider bar to demonstrate the concept of market equilibrium for hamburgers.

Step 4   Create a new graph at the Graphing Workshop *"Try It!"* exercise titled *"Market Equilibrium."* This exercise illustrates how the intersection of the demand and supply curves establishes market equilibrium.

Step 5   Play the *"Causation Chains Game"* titled *"Equilibrium and the Price System."*

Step 6   Read the *EconNews* titled *"The Railroads Are So Busy, They Don't Know if They're Coming or Going."* This article describes factors that are changing the rates charged by railroads.

Step 7   Read the *EconDebate* titled *"Should There be a Market for Human Organs."* This article describes the limited supply of organs problem in the United States.

The Result   By following the steps above, you have learned that the initial equilibrium occurs at the point where the demand curve crosses the supply curve. You also have learned that either a market surplus or shortage provides the mechanism that establishes the equilibrium price and equilibrium quantity.

THE ECONOMIST'S TOOL KIT
Finding the Equilibrium Price and Quantity

Step one: Label the vertical axis as the price per unit of the good or service and the horizontal axis as the quantity of the good or service per time period. Draw a downward-sloping demand curve and label it D. Draw an upward-sloping supply curve and label it S. Label the price where the quantity demanded equals the quantity supplied as P^* and the corresponding quantity as Q^*.

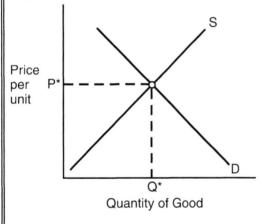

Step two: Choose a price above the equilibrium price and label it P_1. Note that the quantity demanded Q_D is less than the quantity supplied Q_S and there is a surplus. The size of the surplus is the horizontal dotted line between Q_D and Q_S.

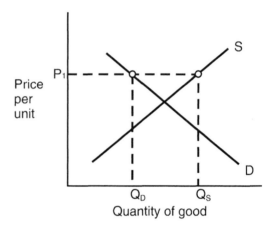

Step three: Choose a price below the equilibrium price and label it P_2. Note that the quantity supplied Q_S is less than the quantity demanded Q_D and there is a shortage. The size of the shortage is the horizontal dotted line between Q_S and Q_D.

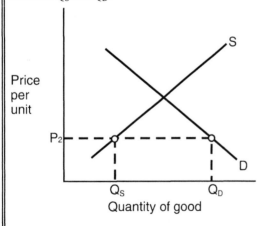

Step four: Note that in a price system without government interference the conditions of surplus and shortage drawn above is only temporary. After a trial-and-error period of time the forces of surplus and shortage will automatically restore the equilibrium price and quantity as originally drawn in step one.

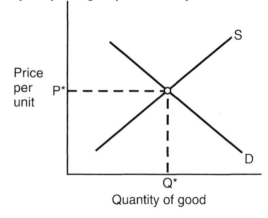

■ COMPLETION QUESTIONS

1. The _____ states that there is an inverse relationship between the price and the quantity demanded, ceteris paribus.

2. A movement along a stationary demand curve caused by a change in price is called a (an) _____.

3. A (an) _____ is one that consumers buy more of when their income increases.

4. _____ states that there is a direct relationship between the price and the quantity supplied, ceteris paribus.

5. A movement along a stationary supply curve in response to a change in price is called a (an) _____.

6. When the price of a good is greater than the equilibrium price, there is an excess quantity supplied called a (an) _____.

7. The unique price and quantity established at the intersection of the supply and demand curves is called _____.

8. The _____ is the supply and demand mechanism which establishes equilibrium through the ability of prices to rise and fall.

9. A (an) _____ is one that there is an inverse relationship between changes in income and its demand curve.

10. A (an) _____ is one that competes with another good for consumer purchases. As a result, there is a direct relationship between a price change for one good and the demand for its "competitor" good.

11. The principle that there is a direct relationship between the price of a good and the quantity sellers are willing to offer for sale in a defined time period, ceteris paribus, is the _____.

12. A (an) _____ is any arrangement in which buyers and sellers interact to determine the price and quantity of goods and services exchanged.

13.   A (an) _____ is one that is jointly consumed with another good. As a result, there is an inverse relationship between a price change for one good and the demand for its "go together" good.

14.   A market condition existing at any price where the quantity supplied is less than the quantity demanded is a (an) _____.

■ MULTIPLE CHOICE

1.   Which of the following is *true* for the law of demand?

   a.   Sellers increase the quantity of a good available as the price of the good increases.
   b.   An increase in price results from false needs.
   c.   There is an inverse relationship between the price of a good and the quantity of the good demanded.
   d.   Prices increase as more units of a product are demanded.

2.   A demand curve for The Steel Porcupines concert tickets would show the:

   a.   quality of service that customers demand when they buy a ticket.
   b.   number of people who like to attend the concert.
   c.   number of tickets the promoters are willing to sell at each price.
   d.   number of concert tickets that will be purchased at each price.

3.   Other things being equal, the effects of an increase in the price of computers would best be represented by which of the following?

   a.   A movement up along the demand curve for computers.
   b.   A movement down along the demand curve for computers.
   c.   A leftward shift in the demand curve for computers.
   d.   A rightward shift in the demand curve for computers.

4.   Which of the following *best* represents the effects of a decrease in the price of tomato juice, other things being equal?

   a.   An upward movement along the demand curve for tomato juice.
   b.   A downward movement along the demand curve for tomato juice.
   c.   A rightward shift in the demand curve for tomato juice.
   d.   A leftward shift in the demand curve for tomato juice.

5. The "ceteris paribus" clause in the law of demand does not allow which of the following factors to change?

    a. Consumer tastes and preferences.
    b. The prices of other goods.
    c. Expectations.
    d. All of the above.

6. Assume that Coca-Cola and Pepsi-Cola are substitutes. A rise in the price of Coca-Cola will have which of the following effects on the market for Pepsi?

    a. A movement down along the Pepsi demand curve.
    b. A rightward shift in the Pepsi demand curve.
    c. A movement up along the Pepsi demand curve.
    d. A leftward shift in the Pepsi demand curve.

7. Assume that crackers and soup are complementary goods. The effect on the soup market of an increase in the price of crackers (other things being equal) would best be described as a (an):

    a. decrease in the quantity of soup demanded.
    b. decrease in the demand for soup.
    c. increase in the quantity of soup demanded.
    d. increase in the demand for soup.

8. Assume that a computer is a normal good. An increase in consumer income, other things being equal, would:

    a. cause an upward movement along the demand curve for computers.
    b. cause a downward movement along the demand curve for computers.
    c. shift the demand curve for computers to the left.
    d. shift the demand curve for computers to the right.

9. Which of the following will increase the demand for large automobiles?

    a. A fall in the price of small automobiles.
    b. A rise in insurance rates for large automobiles.
    c. A fall in the price of large automobiles.
    d. An increase in buyers' incomes (assuming large automobiles to be a normal good).

10.   Assume that brand X is an inferior good and name brand Y is a normal good. An increase in consumer income, other things being equal, will cause a (an):

    a.   upward movement along the demand curve for name brand Y.
    b.   downward movement along the demand curve for brand X.
    c.   rightward shift in the demand curve for brand X.
    d.   leftward shift in the demand curve for brand X.

11.   There is news that the price of Tucker's Root Beer will increase significantly next week. If the demand for Tucker's Root Beer reacts *only* to this factor and shifts to the right, the position of this demand curve has reacted to a change in:

    a.   tastes.
    b.   income levels.
    c.   the price of other goods.
    d.   the number of buyers.
    e.   expectations.

12.   The theory of supply states that:

    a.   there is a negative relationship between the price of a good and the quantity of it purchased by suppliers.
    b.   there is a positive relationship between the price of a good and the quantity that buyers choose to purchase.
    c.   there is a positive relationship between the price of a good and the quantity of it offered for sale by suppliers.
    d.   at a lower price, a greater quantity will be supplied.

13.   Supply curves slope upward because:

    a.   the quality is assumed to vary with price.
    b.   technology improves over time, increasing the ability of firms to produce more at each possible price.
    c.   increases in the price of a good lead to rightward shifts of the supply curve.
    d.   rising prices provide producers with higher profit incentives needed to increase the quantity supplied.

14.   Which of the following will *not* cause a movement along the supply curve?

    a.   Changes in the sellers' expectations.
    b.   Increases in taxes per unit of output.
    c.   Advances in technology.
    d.   All of the above.

15.   Assume that oranges and peaches can both be grown on the same type of land, a decrease in the price of peaches, other things being equal, will cause a (an):

a.   upward movement along the supply curve for oranges.
b.   downward movement along the supply curve for oranges.
c.   rightward shift of the supply curve for oranges.
d.   leftward shift of the supply curve for oranges.

16.   An advance in technology results in:

a.   suppliers offering a larger quantity than before at each given price.
b.   suppliers offering the same quantity as before at a lower price.
c.   a rightward shift of the supply curve.
d.   an increase in supply.
e.   all of the above.

Exhibit 1 Supply for Tucker's Cola data

Quantity supplied per week (millions of gallons)	Price per gallon
6	$3.00
5	2.50
4	2.00
3	1.50
2	1.00
1	.50

17.   As shown in Exhibit 1, the price and quantity supplied by sellers of Tucker's Cola have a (an) _____ relationship.

a.   direct.
b.   inverse.
c.   negative.
d.   zero.

18.   In reference to Exhibit 1, assume the price of Tucker's Cola is $1.00 per gallon. If the price were to rise to $3.00 per gallon, and all other factors, such as taxes, etc. remained constant, the result would be a (an):

   a.   decrease in supply.
   b.   increase in supply.
   c.   decrease in quantity supplied.
   d.   increase in quantity supplied.

19.   Assume Congress passes a new tax of $2.00 per pack on cigarettes. The effect on the supply curve is a (an):

   a.   decrease in supply.
   b.   increase in supply.
   c.   decrease in quantity supplied.
   d.   increase in quantity supplied.

20.   Market equilibrium is defined as:

   a.   the condition in which there is neither a shortage or surplus.
   b.   the condition under which the separately formulated plans of buyers and sellers exactly mesh when tested in the market.
   c.   represented graphically by the intersection of the supply and demand curves.
   d.   all of the above.

Exhibit 2 Supply and demand curves

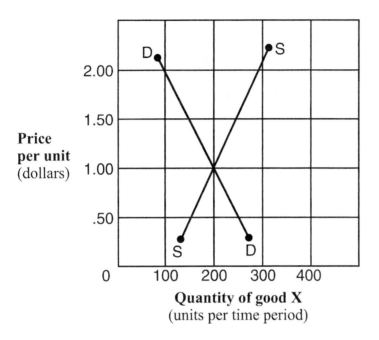

21.   In the market shown in Exhibit 2, the equilibrium price and quantity of good X are:

   a. $0.50, 250.
   b. $2.00, 300.
   c. $2.00, 100.
   d. $1.00, 200.

22.   In Exhibit 2, at a price of $.50 the market for good X will experience a:

   a.   shortage of 100 units.
   b.   surplus of 100 units.
   c.   shortage of 300 units.
   d.   surplus of 200 units.

23.   In Exhibit 2, if the price moves from $2.00 to $1.00, inventories will:

   a.   remain unchanged.
   b.   fall.
   c.   rise.
   d.   fall and then rise.

24.   In Exhibit 2, if the market price of good X is initially $.50, a movement toward equilibrium requires:

   a.   no change, because an equilibrium already exists.
   b.   the price to fall below $.50 and both the quantity supplied and the quantity demanded to rise.
   c.   the price to remain the same, but the supply curve to shift to the left.
   d.   the price to rise above $.50, the quantity supplied to rise, and the quantity demanded to fall.

25.   In Exhibit 2, if the market price of good X is initially $1.50, a movement toward equilibrium requires:

   a.   no change, because an equilibrium already exists.
   b.   the price to fall below $1.50 and both the quantity supplied and the quantity demanded to fall.
   c.   the price to remain the same, but the supply curve to shift to the left.
   d.   the price to fall below $1.50, the quantity supplied to fall, and the quantity demanded to rise.

26.   Three of the four events described below might reasonably be expected to shift the demand curve for beef to a new position. One would *not shift* the demand curve. The single exception is:

   a.   a change in people's tastes with respect to beef.
   b.   an increase in the money income of beef consumers.
   c.   a fall in the price of beef.
   d.   a widespread advertising campaign undertaken by the producers of a product competitive with beef (e.g., pork).

27.   Yesterday Seller A supplied 400 units of a good X at $10 per unit. Today Seller A supplies the same quantity of units at $5 per unit. Based on this evidence, Seller A has experienced a (an):

   a.   decrease in supply.
   b.   increase in supply.
   c.   increase in the quantity supplied.
   d.   decrease in the quantity supplied.
   e.   increase in demand.

28.   Assuming that wheat and corn can both be grown on the same type of land, a decrease in the price of corn, other factors held constant, will cause a (an):

    a.   downward movement along the supply curve for wheat.
    b.   upward movement along the supply curve for wheat.
    c.   rightward shift in the supply curve for wheat.
    d.   leftward shift in the supply curve for wheat.

■ TRUE OR FALSE

1.   T   F   According to the law of demand, if the price of a good increases, other things being equal, the quantity demanded will decrease.

2.   T   F   Other things being equal, an increase in the price of aspirin will decrease the demand for aspirin.

3.   T   F   If a vacation in Paris is a normal good, other things being equal, an increase in consumer income will increase the demand for travel to Paris.

4.   T   F   If people buy more of a generic brand when consumer income falls, it is an inferior good.

5.   T   F   If pork and beans is an inferior good, other things being equal, an increase in consumer income will decrease the demand for pork and beans.

6.   T   F   Suppose A and B are substitute goods. Other things being equal, the demand curve for A will shift to the right when the price of B goes down.

7.   T   F   Suppose A and B are complementary goods. Other things being equal, the demand curve for A will shift to the right when the price of B goes up.

8.   T   F   If input prices increase, the supply curve for cheese will shift to the right.

9.   T   F   Suppose the market price of a good X is below the equilibrium price. The result is a shortage and sellers can be expected to decrease the quantity of that good X supplied.

10.   T   F   A shortage means that the quantity demanded is greater than the quantity supplied at the prevailing price.

11.   T   F   Excess quantity demanded for a good creates pressure to push the price of that good down toward the equilibrium price.

12.   T   F   A surplus means that the quantity supplied is greater than the quantity demanded at the prevailing price.

■ CROSSWORD PUZZLE

Fill in the crossword puzzle from the list of key concepts. Not all of the concepts are used.

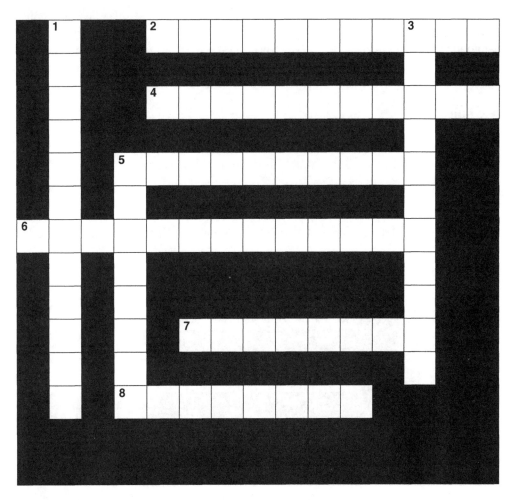

ACROSS

2. The principle that there is a direct relationship between the price of a good and the quantity sellers are willing to offer for sale in a defined time period, ceteris paribus.
4. Any price where the quantity demanded equals the quantity supplied.
5. A competing good.
6. A jointly consumed good.
7. When the quantity demanded exceeds the quantity supplied.
8. A change in the quantity _____ is a movement between points along a stationary demand curve, ceteris paribus.

DOWN

1. A good for which there is an inverse relationship between a change in income and its and its demand curve.
3. A mechanism that creates market equilibrium.
5. A change in the quantity _____ is a movement along a stationary supply curve, ceteris paribus.

■ ANSWERS

Completion Questions

1. law of demand
2. change in quantity demanded
3. normal good
4. law of supply
5. change in quantity supplied
6. surplus
7. equilibrium
8. price system
9. inferior good
10. substitute good
11. law of supply
12. market
13. complementary good
14. shortage

Multiple Choice

1. c 2. d 3. a 4. b 5. d 6. b 7. b 8. d 9. d 10. d 11. e 12. c 13. d 14. d 15. c 16. e 17. a 18. d 19. a 20. d 21. d 22. a 23. b 24. d 25. d 26. c 27. b 28. c

True or False

1. True 2. False 3. True 4. True 5. True 6. False 7. False 8. False 9. False 10. True 11. False 12. True

Crossword Puzzle

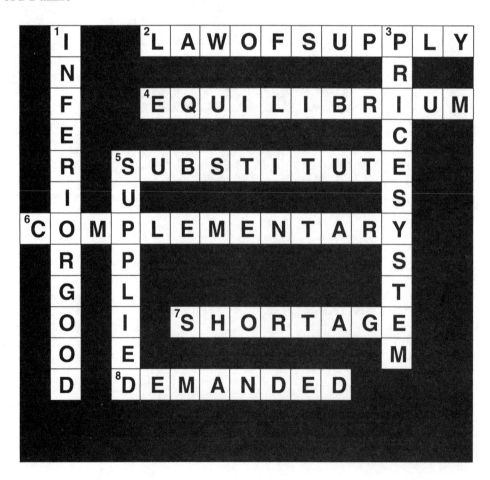

Chapter 4
Markets in Action

■ **CHAPTER IN A NUTSHELL**

Chapter 4 builds on the basic supply and demand model introduced in the previous chapter. Here the focus is on how equilibrium prices and quantities change when other factors change. Applications in the chapter, for example, to Caribbean cruises, video rentals, lumber, and oat bran are included to help you understand and appreciate the basics of supply and demand analysis. This chapter also explains what happens when the government sets price floors or ceilings and therefore prices do not adjust to the equilibrium price. The chapter concludes with an introduction to the concept of market failure that is concerned with how the price system functions when it fails. Four cases of market failure discussed are: lack of competition, externalities, public goods, and income inequality.

■ **KEY CONCEPTS**

Externality
Market failure
Price ceiling

Price floor
Public good

■ **MASTER THE LEARNING OBJECTIVES**

Please visit the Tucker Xtra! site at http://tuckerxtra.swlearning.com to find the interactive version of the "Master the Learning Objectives" feature.

#1 - Understand how an increase or decrease in the demand curve or supply curve changes the equilibrium price and quantity.

Step 1   Read the section in your textbook titled *"Changes in Market Equilibrium."* After reading this section, you should be able to use a graph and describe changes in market equilibrium.

Step 2   Watch the Graphing Workshop *"See It!"* tutorial titled *"Market Equilibrium."* Study how changes in the demand curve and supply curve affect the equilibrium prices and quantity of milk.

Step 3   Create a new graph at the Graphing Workshop *"Try It!"* exercise titled *"Market Equilibrium."* This exercise illustrates how a change in the demand curve or supply curve establishes a new market equilibrium price and quantity.

Step 4   Play the *"Causation Chains Game"* titled *"The Effect of Shifts in Demand on Market Equilibrium."*

Step 5   Play the *"Causation Chains Game"* titled *"The Effects of Shifts in Supply on Market Equilibrium."*

Step 6   Listen to the *"Ask the Instructor Video Clip"* titled *"What Factors Affect the Auction Price of Your House?"* You will learn demand and supply factors that affect the price of a house.

Step 7   Listen to the *"Ask the Instructor Video Clip"* titled *"Why Do Some Prices Adjust More Slowly?"* You will learn how equilibrium prices adjust in the market for stocks and nurses.

Step 8   Watch the *CNN Video Clip* titled *"Red Light for Mexican Drug Traffickers"* and analyze the impact of actions by the Mexican government on the price of illegal drugs.

Step 9   Watch the *CNN Video Clip* titled *"Oil Creates Troubled Waters"* and analyze the reasons for higher gas prices due to changes in demand and supply.

Step 10   Watch the *CNN Video Clip* titled *"Exploring Higher Gas Prices"* and analyze the reasons for higher gasoline prices due to changes in demand and supply.

Step 11   Read the *EconNews* article titled *"Can You Help Out Economics Ph.D.'s Who Are Down on Their Luck?"* This article describes how supply and demand curves affected Ph.D. salaries.

The Result   By following these steps, you have learned that the equilibrium price and quantity change as a result of shifts in either the demand or supply curves.

#2 - Explain the impact of a price ceiling and a price floor set in a market by the government.

Step 1   Read the section in your textbook titled *"Can the Law of Supply and Demand Be Repealed?"* After reading this section, you should be able to use a graph and describe the effects of a price ceiling or a price floor.

Step 2   Read the Graphing Workshop *"Grasp It!"* tutorial titled *"Price Controls."* This exercise uses a slider bar to demonstrate the impact of rent controls (price ceiling) and the minimum wage (price floor).

Step 3   Create a new graph at the Graphing Workshop *"Try It!"* exercise titled *"Price Controls."* This exercise illustrates the impact of price controls on the market for gasoline.

Step 4   Play the *"Causation Chains Game"* titled *"Rent Control."*

Step 5   Play the *"Causation Chains Game"* titled *"The Minimum Wage."*

Step 6   Listen to the *"Ask the Instructor Video Clip"* titled *"Do the Terms 'Shortage' and 'Scarcity' Mean the Same Thing?"* You will learn that price controls cause shortages.

Step 7   Read the *EconDebate* titled *"Does an Increase in the Minimum Wage Result in a High Unemployment Rate?"* This article describes the impact of the minimum wage using supply and demand analysis.

Step 8   Read the *EconDebate* titled *"Time to End Rent Control in New York."* This article describes the debate over rent control in New York City.

The Result By following these steps, you have learned that a price ceiling or a price floor set by government can cause a shortage or surplus to persist in the market.

#3 - Describe what is meant by market failure and how government attempts to correct market failure.

Step 1   Read the section in your textbook titled *"Market Failure."* After reading this section, you should be able to explain different types of market failure.

Step 2   Read the Graphing Workshop *"Grasp It!"* exercise titled *"Externalities."* This exercise uses a slider bar to demonstrate the concept of negative and positive externalities.

Step 3   Create a new graph at the Graphing Workshop *"Try It!"* exercise titled *"Externalities."* This exercise illustrates the market for gasoline and the impact of air pollution.

Step 4   Listen to the *"Ask the Instructor Video Clip"* titled *"How Does Government Affect the Economy?"* You will learn how pollution and solutions to pollution affect the equilibrium and quantity of a good.

Step 5   Listen to the *"Ask the Instructor Video Clip"* titled *"What Does Barbed Wire Have to Do with Externalities?"* You will learn to use the concept of externalities to explain the conflict between ranchers and farmers.

Step 6   Listen to the *"Ask the Instructor Video Clip"* titled *"What Is the Meaning of Public Goods?"* You will learn the difference between public and private goods.

Step 7   Listen to the *"Ask the Instructor Video Clip"* titled *"How Do Educational Vouchers Relate to Market Structure?"* You will learn how vouchers can be used for school choice.

Step 8   Read the *EconDebate* titled *"Do School Vouchers Improve the Quality of Education?"* This article describes the history and arguments concerning using educational vouchers.

The Result   By following the steps above, you have learned that external costs and benefits cause an overallocation or underallocation of resources.

THE ECONOMIST'S TOOL KIT
Comparing the Effects of Changes in Demand and Supply

Step one: Increase demand and note that both the equilibrium price and quantity increase.

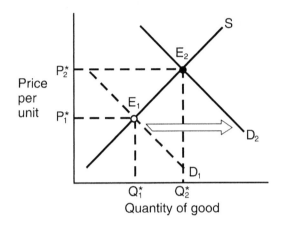

Step two: Decrease demand and note that both the equilibrium price and quantity decrease.

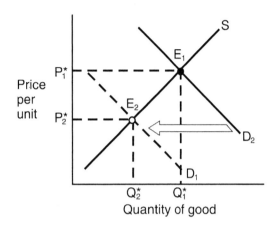

Step three: Increase supply and note that the equilibrium price decreases and the equilibrium quantity increases.

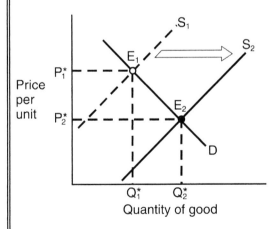

Step four: Decrease supply and note that the equilibrium price increases and the equilibrium quantity decreases.

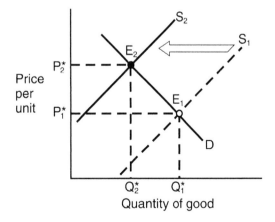

■ COMPLETION QUESTIONS

1.   A (an) _____ is a maximum price mandated by government.

2.   A (an) _____ is a minimum legal price mandated by government.

3.   Pollution is an example of _____ which means too many resources are used to produce the product responsible for the pollution. Two basic approaches to solve this market failure are regulation and pollution taxes.

4.   Vaccination shots provide _____ which means sellers devote too few resources to produce this product. Two basic solutions to this type of market failure are laws to require consumption of shots and special subsidies.

5.   A (an) _____ is consumed by everyone regardless of whether they pay for them or not. National defense and air traffic control are examples.

6.   _____ means the price system fails to efficiently allocate resources in the production of output.

7.   A (an) _____ is a cost or benefit imposed on people other than the consumers and producers of a good or service.

■ MULTIPLE CHOICE

Exhibit 1 Supply and demand curves

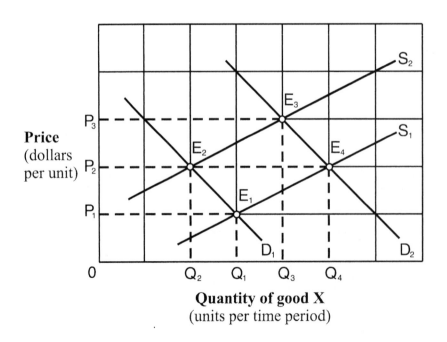

Quantity of good X
(units per time period)

1.   Initially the market shown in Exhibit 1 is in equilibrium at P2, Q2 (E2). Changes in market conditions result in a new equilibrium at P2, Q4 (E4). This change is stated as a (an):

   a.   increase in supply and an increase in demand.
   b.   increase in supply and a decrease in demand.
   c.   decrease in demand and a decrease in supply.
   d.   increase in demand and an increase in quantity supplied.

2.   Initially the market shown in Exhibit 1 is in equilibrium at P_3, Q_3 (E_3). Changes in market conditions result in a new equilibrium at P_2, Q_2 (E_2). This change is stated as a (an):

   a.   decrease in demand and an increase in supply.
   b.   decrease in demand and a decrease in quantity supplied.
   c.   decrease in quantity demanded and an increase in quantity supplied.
   d.   decrease in quantity demanded and an increase in supply.

3.   In Exhibit 1, which of the following would *not* cause a shift from S_1 to S_2?

   a.   An increase in input prices.
   b.   A rise in the price of other goods.
   c.   An increase in taxes per unit.
   d.   An increase in consumer income.

4.   The market shown in Exhibit 1 is initially in equilibrium at point E_4. Union negotiations result in a wage increase. Other things being equal, which of the following is the new equilibrium after this wage increase is in effect?

   a. E_1.
   b. E_2.
   c. E_3.
   d. E_4.

5.   The market shown in Exhibit 1 is initially in equilibrium at E_4. Changes in market conditions result in a new equilibrium at E_3. This change is stated as a (an):

   a.   increase in supply and an increase in quantity demanded.
   b.   increase in supply and a decrease in demand.
   c.   decrease in supply and a decrease in quantity demanded.
   d.   increase in demand an increase in supply.

6. In Exhibit 1, an increase in demand would cause a move from which equilibrium point to another, other things being equal?

    a. E_1 to E_2.
    b. E_1 to E_3.
    c. E_4 to E_1.
    d. E_1 to E_4.

7. In Exhibit 1, an increase in quantity supplied would cause a move from which equilibrium point to another, other things being equal?

    a. E_1 to E_2.
    b. E_1 to E_4.
    c. E_4 to E_1.
    d. E_3 to E_4.

8. Beginning from an equilibrium at point E_2 in Exhibit 1, an increase in demand for good X, other things being equal, would move the equilibrium point to:

    a. E_1, no change.
    b. E_2.
    c. E_3.
    d. E_4.

9. Suppose a price ceiling is set by the government below the market equilibrium price. Which of the following will result?

    a. The demand curve will shift to the left.
    b. The quantity demanded will exceed the quantity supplied.
    c. The quantity supplied will exceed the quantity demanded.
    d. There will be a surplus.

10. Suppose a price floor is set by the government above the market equilibrium price. Which of the following will result?

    a. There will be a surplus.
    b. The quantity demanded will exceed the quantity supplied.
    c. The demand curve will shift to the left.
    d. None of the above.

11.   Suppose the government imposes rent control (a price ceiling) below the equilibrium price for rental housing. Which of the following will result?

a.   Black markets.
b.   The quality of existing rental housing deteriorates.
c.   Shortages.
d.   All of the above.

12.   If the equilibrium price of good X is $5 and a price ceiling is imposed at $4, the eventual result will be a (an):

a.   accumulation of inventories of unsold gas.
b.   shortage.
c.   surplus.
d.   all of the above.

13.   The former Soviet Union was known for black markets. An explanation for the existence of the black market is that:

a.   goods were not subject to price controls.
b.   the government imposed a price floor below the equilibrium price.
c.   the government imposed a price ceiling below the equilibrium price.
d.   all of the above.

Exhibit 2 Data on supply and demand

Bushels Demanded per month	Price per Bushel	Bushels Supplied per Month
45	$5	77
50	4	73
56	3	68
61	2	61
67	1	57

14.   In Exhibit 2, the equilibrium price per bushel of wheat is:

a. $1.
b. $2.
c. $3.
d. $4.

15.   Which of the following would occur if the government imposed a price floor (support price) of $4 per bushel in the wheat market shown in Exhibit 2?

a.   Buyers would want to purchase more wheat than is supplied.
b.   Buyers would not purchase all of the wheat grown.
c.   Shortage of wheat would increase the price of wheat.
d.   Farmers would grow less wheat.

16.   Which of the following is an example of market failure?

a.   Public goods.
b.   Externalities.
c.   Lack of competition.
d.   All of the above.

17.   A good that provides external benefits to society has:

a.   too few resources devoted to its production.
b.   too many resources devoted to its production.
c.   the optimal resources devoted to its production.
d.   not provided profits to producers of the good.

18.   Which of the following is a property of a public good?

a.   A public good is free from externalities.
b.   Many individuals benefit simultaneously.
c.   A public good is not subject to free riders.
d.   A public good is established by law.

19.   Which of the following is a public good?

a.   Air traffic control.
b.   National defense.
c.   Clean air.
d.   All of the above.

20.   Price ceilings are imposed if the government believes:

a.   the market will not achieve an equilibrium price.
b.   the market equilibrium price is too low.
c.   an excess supply of the product exists.
d.   the market equilibrium price is too high.
e.   the quantity demanded will less than the quantity supplied of the product.

21.   A third party is:

    a.   the party to which a contractual agreement is meant to benefit.
    b.   a person, or persons, who are unintentionally affected by the actions of others.
    c.   the third person in a three-way contract.
    d.   the person who owns the property right in a contract.
    e.   when the government attempts to mediate a dispute between management and labor.

■ TRUE OR FALSE

1.   T   F   In a market without government interference, the price is free to move the equilibrium.

2.   T   F   An equilibrium price is unaffected by nonprice factors.

3.   T   F   If the demand curve increases while the supply curve remains unchanged, the equilibrium price would decrease.

4.   T   F   If the supply curve decreases while the demand curve remains unchanged, the equilibrium price would decrease.

5.   T   F   Assume a ceiling price is set above the equilibrium price. The result is a shortage.

6.   T   F   Assume a price floor is set above the equilibrium price. The result is a surplus.

7.   T   F   A public good is any good or service that users collectively consume and there is no way to bar free riders.

8.   T   F   It's difficult for a private firm to provide a public good because of free riders.

■ CROSSWORD PUZZLE

Fill in the crossword puzzle from the list of key concepts. Not all of the concepts are used.

ACROSS

7.   Vaccinations.

DOWN

1.   A maximum price set by the government.
2.   Pollution.
3.   A situation in which the price system creates a problem for society or fails to achieve society's goals.
4.   A cost or benefit imposed on people.
5.   A minimum price set by the government.
6.   A good with a free rider problem.

■ ANSWERS

Completion Questions

1. price ceiling
2. price floor
3. external cost
4. external benefits
5. public good
6. market failure
7. externality

Multiple Choice

1. a 2. b 3. d 4. c 5. c 6. d 7. b 8. c 9. b 10. a 11. d 2. b 13. c 14. b 15. b 16. d 17. a 18. b 19. d 20. d 21. a 22. b

True or False

1. True 2. False 3. False 4. False 5. False 6. True 7. True 8. True

Crossword Puzzle

Chapter 5
Gross Domestic Product

■ CHAPTER IN A NUTSHELL

This chapter introduces you to national income accounting. It is important because it provides the foundation for understanding macroeconomics. The central macroeconomic variable is gross domestic product (GDP), which is the standard measure of the economy's output. The circular flow model separates GDP into markets for products, markets for resources, consumers spending and consumers earning money. Using the expenditure approach, GDP equals the total amount spent on final goods and services. Total spending (GDP) is broken down into four parts: consumption (C), investment (I), government spending (G), and net exports (X-M). A second approach to measuring GDP is the income approach. Using this technique, GDP equals the sum of compensation of employers, rents, profits, net interest, indirect business taxes, and depreciation. Other measures of the economy include: National Income (NI), Personal Income (PI), and Disposable Personal Income (DI). The chapter concludes with an explanation for using the GDP deflator to calculate real GDP by removing inflation from nominal GDP.

■ KEY CONCEPTS

Circular flow model

Disposable personal
   income (DI)

Expenditure approach

Final goods

Flow

GDP chain price index

Gross domestic product (GDP)

Gross national product (GNP)

Indirect business taxes

Intermediate goods

National Income

Nominal GDP

Personal income (PI)

Real GDP

Transfer payment

■ MASTER THE LEARNING OBJECTIVES

Please visit the Tucker Xtra! site at http://tuckerxtra.swlearning.com to find the interactive version of the "Master the Learning Objectives" feature.

#1 - Understand how gross domestic product (GDP) is computed.

Step 1   Read the sections in your textbook titled *"Gross Domestic Product," "The Expenditure Approach," "The Income Approach," "GDPs in Other Countries,"* and *"Other National Accounts."*

Step 2   Read the *EconNews* article titled *"Long-Run Importance of the Service Sector."* This article describes the three components of consumer spending.

Step 3   Read the *EconNews* article titled *"Rapid Economic Growth Reported."* This article describes how GDP is calculated.

The Result   Following these steps, you have learned that GDP measures the total spending in a country for consumption (C), investment (I), government spending (G), and exports minus imports (X - M).

#2 - Understand shortcomings of GDP.

Step 1   Read the section in your textbook titled *"GDP Shortcomings."*

Step 2   Listen to the *"Ask the Instructor Video Clip"* titled *"What Is Included in the Calculation of GDP?"* You will learn GDP shortcomings.

Step 3   Read the *EconNews* article titled *"How Domestic is GDP?"* This article describes GDP shortcomings.

The Result   Following these steps, you have learned that GDP is a less-than-perfect computation that omits certain measures of economic activity.

#3 - Compute real gross domestic product.

Step 1   Read the section in your textbook titled *"Changing Nominal GDP to Real GDP."*

Step 3   Step 2 Listen to the *"Ask the Instructor Video Clip"* titled *"Was There a Recession in 1974?"* You will learn the importance of the difference between nominal and real GDP.

The Result   Following these steps, you have learned how to convert nominal GDP to real GDP and understand that real GDP is used to measure changes in GDP over time because it adjusts for inflation.

■ COMPLETION QUESTIONS

1. _____ is the most widely used measure of a nation's economic performance and is the market value of all final goods produced in the United States during a period of time.

2. To avoid double counting, GDP does not include _____.

3. The _____ is a diagram representing the flow of products and resources between businesses and households in exchange for money payments.

4. The _____ sums the four major spending components of GDP consisting of: consumption, investment, government, and net exports.

5. _____ include general sales taxes, excise taxes, and customs duties.

6. _____ is total income received by households and is calculated as national income less corporate taxes, retained earnings, Social Security taxes plus transfer payments and net interest from government securities.

7. _____ is personal income minus personal taxes.

8. _____ measures all final goods produced in a given time period valued at the prices existing during the time period of production.

9. _____ is the value of all final goods and services produced during any time period valued at prices existing in a base year.

10. _____ is the market value of all final goods and services produced by a nation's residents no matter where they are located.

11. A government payment to individuals not in exchange for goods or services currently produced is called a _____.

12. _____ are finished goods and services produced for the ultimate user.

13. A _____ is a quantity that exists at a given point in time measured in dollars.

14.   A _____ is a measurement in units per time period such as dollars per year. For example, income and consumption can be measured per week, per month, or per year.

15.   The national income account method that measures GDP by adding all incomes, including compensation of employees, rents, net interest, and profits is called the

_____ .

16.   The _____ is a measure that compares changes in the prices of all final goods during a given year to the prices of those goods in a base year.

■ MULTIPLE CHOICE

1.   Gross domestic product (GDP) is defined as:

a.   the market value of all final goods and services produced within the borders of a nation.
b.   incomes received by all a nation's households.
c.   the quantity of each good and service produced by U.S. residents.
d.   none of the above.

2.   Gross domestic product (GDP) does *not* include:

a.   used goods sold in the current time period.
b.   foreign produced goods.
c.   intermediate as well as final goods.
d.   All of the above would *not* be included.

3.   The lower portion of the circular flow model contains factor markets in which households provide:

a.   output of all final goods and services produced.
b.   savings, spending, and investment.
c.   labor, money, and machines.
d.   land, labor, and capital.

Exhibit 1 Expenditure approach

National income account	(billions of dollars)
Personal consumption expenditures (C)	$1,000
Net exports (X-M)	100
Federal government consumption and gross investment expenditures (G)	200
State and local government consumption and gross investment expenditures (G)	400
Imports	20
Gross private domestic investment (I)	75

4.   As shown in Exhibit 1, total expenditures by households for domestically produced goods is:

   a. $1,000 billion.
   b. $100 billion.
   c. $600 billion.
   d. $20 billion.

5.   As shown in Exhibit 1, total expenditures by businesses for fixed investment (capital) and inventories is:

   a. $1,000 billion.
   b. $100 billion.
   c. $400 billion.
   d. $20 billion
   e. $75 billion.

6.   As shown in Exhibit 1, GDP is _____.

   a. $1,000 billion
   b. $1,500 billion
   c. $1,775 billion
   d. $2,000 billion

Exhibit 2 Income approach

National income account	(billions of dollars)
Depreciation	$ 500
Net interest	2,000
Compensation of employees	6,000
Profits	1,500
Rental income	200
Indirect business taxes	800

7.   As shown in Exhibit 2, gross domestic product (GDP) is:

a. $8,000 billion.
b. $8,800 billion.
c. $9,400 billion.
d. $11,000 billion.
e.   None of the above.

8.   As shown in Exhibit 2, national income (NI) is:

a. $9,000 billion.
b. $9,700 billion.
c. $10,200 billion.
d. $11,000 billion.
e.   None of the above.

9.   GDP does count:

a.   state and local government purchases.
b.   spending for new homes.
c.   changes in inventories.
d.   none of the above.
e.   all of the above.

10. Personal income is:

  a. national income minus transfer payments, net interest, and dividends.
  b. the amount households have available only for consumption.
  c. total income earned by households before taxes.
  d. all of the above.
  e. none of the above.

11. The equation for determining real GDP for year X is:

  a. $\dfrac{\text{nominal GDP for year X} \times 100}{\text{average family income}}$.

  b. $\dfrac{\text{nominal GDP for year X} - 100}{\text{GDP for year X}}$.

  c. $\dfrac{\text{nominal GDP for year X}}{\text{average nominal GDP}}$.

  d. none of the above.

12. Suppose U.S. nominal GDP was $7,500 billion in 1997 and the GDP chain price index is 120.0. Real GDP in constant 1992 dollars is:

  a. $5,488 billion.
  b. $6,250 billion.
  c. $6,740 billion.
  d. $7,789 billion.

13. If we computed GDP using the expenditure approach, and then computed it using the income approach, which of the following can be expected to be true?

  a. GDP computed from the expenditure approach will be larger than when GDP is computed using the income approach.
  b. GDP computed from the expenditure approach will be equal to GDP computed using the income approach.
  c. GDP computed from the expenditure approach will be smaller than when GDP is computed using the income approach.
  d. None of the above is correct.

14.   Which of the following correctly gives us national income (NI)?

    a.   Gross domestic product minus depreciation.
    b.   Personal income minus personal taxes.
    c.   Net national product minus indirect business taxes.
    d.   Consumption plus investment plus government plus net exports.

15.   Which national income account should be examined to discover trends in the after-tax income that people have to save and spend?

    a.   Gross domestic product (GDP).
    b.   Gross national product (GNP).
    c.   National income (NI).
    d.   Disposable personal income (DI).

16.   Which of the following is a shortcoming of GDP?

    a.   GDP excludes changes in inventories.
    b.   GDP includes an estimate of illegal transactions.
    c.   GDP excludes nonmarket transactions.
    d.   GDP includes business investment spending.

17.   National income is officially measured by adding:

    a.   the quantity of each final good and service produced valued at its market price.
    b.   the total of all expenditures on newly produced final goods and services $(GDP = C + I + H)$.
    c.   the total of all incomes earned by households from the sale of factors of production.
    d.   capital consumption allowance and gross domestic product $(GDP + CCA = NNP)$.

18.   Which of the following is included in personal income but *not* in national income?

    a.   Compensation for workers.
    b.   Proprietors' income.
    c.   Corporate profits.
    d.   Social Security payments.
    e.   Rent.

■ TRUE OR FALSE

1.   T   F   Gross domestic product is the total dollar value at current prices of all final and intermediate goods produced by a nation during a given time period.

2.   T   F   The circular flow model illustrates that aggregate spending in the product markets equals 70 percent of aggregate income earned in the factor markets.

3.   T   F   Personal consumption expenditures is the largest component of total spending.

4.   T   F   Fixed investment is the dollar amount businesses are adding to our nation's amount of plant and equipment.

5.   T   F   Gross domestic product (GDP) is a satisfactory measure of both economic "goods" and "bads".

6.   T   F   The difference between gross domestic product and national income is an estimate of the depreciation of fixed capital.

7.   T   F   Nominal values are values measured in terms of the prices at which goods and services are actually sold.

8.   T   F   All changes in nominal GDP are due to price changes.

9.   T   F   If the GDP chain price index in a given year is less than 100, real GDP in that year would be greater than nominal GDP.

10.   T   F   A GDP price chain price index number of 120.0 for a given year indicates that prices in that year are 20 percent higher than prices in the base year.

11.   T   F   Over time, nominal GDP rises faster than real GDP because of the effects of inflation as measured by the GDP chain price index.

12.   T   F   In any year, nominal GDP divided by the GDP chain price index multiplied by 100 equals real GDP.

■ CROSSWORD PUZZLE

Fill in the crossword puzzle from the list of key concepts. Not all of the concepts are used.

ACROSS

4.   _____ business taxes are levied as a percentage of the prices of goods sold and therefore collected as part of the firm's revenue.

6.   The _____ national product is the market value of all final goods and services produced by a nation's residents no matter where they are located.

8.   _____ GDP is the value of all final goods based on the prices existing during the time period of production.

9.   _____ goods and services used as inputs for the production of final goods.

10.   Finished goods and services produced for the ultimate user.

12.   _____ GDP is the value of all final goods produced during a given time period based on the prices existing in a selected base year.

DOWN

1.   _____ approach is a broad price index which measure changes in prices of consumer goods, business, construction, government spending, exports, and imports.

2.   The _____ flow model is a diagram showing the flow of products from businesses to households and the flow of resources from households to businesses.

3.   Gross _____ product is the market value of all final goods and services produced in a nation during a period of time usually a year.

5.   _____ personal income is the amount that households actually have to spend or save after payment of personal taxes.

7.   The GDP _____ price index is a measure that compares changes in the prices of all final goods during a given year to the prices of those goods in a base year.

11.   _____ is the gross domestic product minus depreciation of capital worn out in producing output.

■ ANSWERS

Completion Questions

1. gross domestic product (GDP)
2. intermediate goods
3. circular flow model
4. expenditure approach
5. indirect business taxes
6. personal income
7. disposable personal income
8. nominal GDP
9. real GDP
10. gross national product (GNP)
11. transfer payment
12. final goods
13. stock
14. flow
15. income approach
16. GDP price chain index

Multiple Choice

1. a 2. d 3. d 4. a 5. e 6. c 7. d 8. b 9. e 10. e 11. d 12. b 13. b 14. c 15. d 16. c 17. c 18. d

True or False

1. False 2. False 3. True 4. True 5. False 6. True 7. True 8. False 9. True 10. True 11. True 12. True

Crossword Puzzle

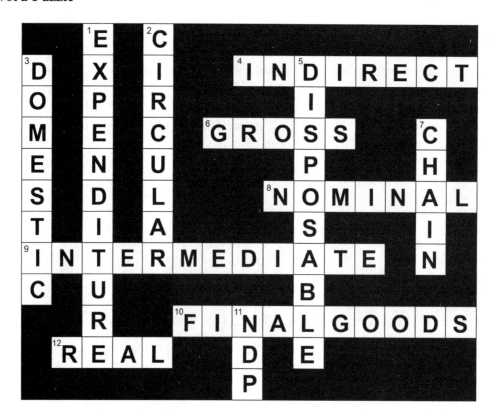

Chapter 6
Business Cycles and Unemployment

■ CHAPTER IN A NUTSHELL

Over time real GDP rises and falls. These upswings and downswings are called the business cycle. Each cycle can be divided into four phases: peak, recession, trough, and recovery. Historical data is presented that shows the long-term trend in real GDP growth is about 3 percent since 1929. The government's chief forecasting gauge for business cycles is the index of leading indicators. The cause of the basic cycle is variation in total spending by households, businesses, government, and foreign buyers. Expressed as a formula: GDP = C + I + G + (X - M).

The text explains how to calculate the unemployment rate and then turns to some criticisms of the unemployment rate. The chapter concludes with a distinction between four types of unemployment: seasonal, frictional, structural, and cyclical. Full employment occurs when the unemployment rate is equal to the sum of the seasonal frictional and structural unemployment rates. The GDP gap is the difference between full-employment real GDP and actual real GDP.

■ KEY CONCEPTS

Business cycle	Lagging indicators
Coincident indicators	Leading indicators
Cyclical unemployment	Peak
Discouraged worker	Recession
Economic growth	Recovery
Frictional unemployment	Seasonal unemployment
Full unemployment	Structural unemployment
GDP gap	Trough
Labor force	Unemployment rate

■ MASTER THE LEARNING OBJECTIVES

Please visit the Tucker Xtra! site at http://tuckerxtra.swlearning.com to find the interactive version of the "Master the Learning Objectives" feature.

#1 - Describe the four phases of the business cycle, business cycle indicators, and interpret economic growth using the change in real GDP.

Step 1   Read the sections in your textbook titled *"The Business-Cycle Roller Coaster"* and *"Total Spending and the Business Cycle."*

Step 2   Listen to the *"Ask the Instructor Video Clip"* titled *"Is A Recession Inevitable After A War?"* You will learn the history of war and recessions in the United States in terms of total spending.

Step 3   Watch the *CNN Video Clip* titled *"Food for Forecasters"* and analyze the factors that result in declines in real GDP.

Step 4   Watch the *CNN Video Clip* titled *"Consumer Tales"* and analyze why changes in consumer confidence concern economists.

The Result   Following these steps, you have learned that there are four phases to the business cycle (peak, recession, trough, and recovery), and there are three business-cycle indicators (leading, coincident, and lagging). You also learned that the long-term annual growth rate of real GDP in the United States since 1929 is about 3 percent.

#2 - Compute the unemployment rate and discuss the difference between frictional, structural, and cyclical types of unemployment.

Step 1   Read the section in your textbook titled *"Unemployment,"* *"Types of Unemployment,"* *"The Goal of Full Employment,"* and *"The GDP Gap."*

Step 2   Listen to the *"Ask the Instructor Video Clip"* titled *"What Are the Four Types of Unemployment?"* You will learn definitions of the types of unemployment.

Step 3   Watch the *CNN Video Clip* titled *"Hires and Fires"* and analyze how monthly employment data indicates economic performance.

Step 4   Read the *EconNews* article titled *"Matching Jobs and Workers."* This article describes discouraged workers.

Step 5   Read the *EconNews* article titled *"The ABC's of Counting."* This article describes the meaning of "seasonably adjusted" data.

Step 6   Read the *EconNews* article titled *"Why Should the Government Help?"* This article describes the Employment Act of 1946 and its importance.

Step 7   Read the *EconNews* article titled *"The Long Run Effect of Offshoring Jobs in Technology."* This article describes the effect of technology on unemployment in the United States.

Step 8   Read the *EconDebate* article titled *"Is a Jobless Recovery a Necessary Part of the New Economy?"* This article describes the issue of the impact of the business cycle and technological change on the unemployment rate.

Step 9   Read the *EconDebate* article titled *"Do Technological Advances Result in Higher Unemployment?"* This article describes the debate concerning the impact of technology on unemployment.

The Result   Following these steps, you have learned that the unemployment rate is the percentage of the civilian labor force that is unemployed. You have also learned that frictional unemployment is short term while workers seek available jobs. Structural unemployment is longer than requiring training for available jobs. Cyclical unemployment is caused by jobs lost during a recession. Also, full employment is achieved when there is only frictional and structural unemployment and no cyclical unemployment exists.

■ COMPLETION QUESTIONS

1.   Recurrent rises and falls in real GDP over a period of years is called the
        _____.

2.   A (an) _____ is officially defined as two consecutive quarters of real GDP decline.

3.   _____ is measured by the annual percentage change in real GDP in a nation.

4.   Economic variables that change at the same time as real GDP changes are called
        _____.

5.   The nation's _____ consists of people who are employed plus those who are out of work but seeking employment.

6.   _____ are persons who want to work, but who have given up.

7.   _____ results from workers who are seeking new jobs that exist.

8.   _____ is unemployment caused by factors in the economy including lack of skills, changes in product demand, or technological change.

9.   The _____ unemployment rate is unemployment resulting from insufficient aggregate demand.

10.   _____ is equal to the total of the frictional and structural unemployment rates.

11.   The _____ is the difference between full-employment or potential real GDP and actual real GDP.

12.   The phase of the business cycle during which real GDP reaches its maximum after rising during a recovery is called a _____.

13.   A _____ is a phase of the business cycle during which real GDP reaches its minimum after falling during a recession.

14.   An upturn in the business cycle during which real GDP rises is called a _____.

15.   _____ are variables that change before real GDP changes.

16.   _____ is the percentage of people in the labor force who are without jobs and are actively seeking jobs.

17.   Variables that change at the same time that real GDP changes are called _____.

18.   _____ is caused by recurring changes in hiring due to changes in weather conditions.

19.   Variables that change after real GDP changes are called _____.

■ MULTIPLE CHOICE

1.   A business cycle is the period of time in which:

a.   a business is established and ceases operations.
b.   there are three phases which are: peak, depression, and recovery.
c.   real GDP declines.
d.   expansion and contraction of economic activity are equal.
e.   none of the above.

2.   The _____ phase of the business cycle follows a recession.

    a.   recovery.
    b.   recession.
    c.   peak.
    d.   trough.

3.   Variables that change before real GDP changes are measured by the:

    a.   personal income index.
    b.   real GDP index.
    c.   forecasting gauge.
    d.   index of leading indicators.

4.   Which of the following is a lagging indicator?

    a.   Outstanding commercial loans.
    b.   Duration of unemployment.
    c.   Prime rate.
    d.   None of the above.
    e.   All of the above.

5.   The civilian labor force consists of:

    a.   civilians who are not in prisons or mental hospitals.
    b.   only individuals who are actually at work during a given week.
    c.   all civilians over the age of 16.
    d.   none of the above.

6.   A criticism of the unemployment rate is that:

    a.   underemployment is measured in the calculation.
    b.   the data includes part-time workers as fully employed.
    c.   discouraged workers are included in the calculation.
    d.   all of the above are problems.

7.   The number of people officially unemployed is *not* the same as the number of people who can't find a job because:

    a.   people who have jobs continue to look for better ones.
    b.   the armed forces is included.
    c.   discourages workers are not counted.
    d.   none of the above.
    e.   all of the above.

8.   Frictional unemployment refers to:

    a.   unemployment related to the ups and downs of the business cycle.
    b.   workers who are between jobs.
    c.   people who spend relatively long periods out of work.
    d.   people who are out of work and have no job skills.

9.   A mismatch of the skills of unemployed workers and the skills required for existing jobs is defined as:

    a.   involuntary unemployment.
    b.   cyclical unemployment.
    c.   structural unemployment.
    d.   frictional unemployment.

10.   Unemployment caused by a recession is called:

    a.   structural unemployment.
    b.   frictional unemployment.
    c.   involuntary unemployment.
    d.   cyclical unemployment.

11.   Full employment occurs when the rate of unemployment consists of:

    a.   structural plus frictional unemployment.
    b.   cyclical plus frictional unemployment.
    c.   structural, frictional, and cyclical unemployment.
    d.   none of the above.

12.   The GDP gap is the difference between:

    a.   frictional unemployment and actual real GDP.
    b.   unemployment rate and real GDP deflator.
    c.   full-employment real GDP and actual real GDP.
    d.   full-employment real GDP and real GDP deflator.

13.   A recession is a business contraction lasting at least:

    a.   one year.
    b.   six months.
    c.   three months.
    d.   one month.

14.   Which of the following is the correct formula for determining the civilian unemployment rate?

    a.   [(the number of unemployed, working-age civilian seeking work)/(the number of civilians in the labor force)] x 100.
    b.   C + I + G + (X-M).
    c.   The total number of unemployed, working-age civilians seeking work.
    d.   (The number of civilians in the labor force) x 100.

15.   When is the GDP gap largest?

    a.   During peak periods in the business cycle.
    b.   During trough periods in the business cycle.
    c.   When unemployment rates are relatively low.
    d.   When cyclical unemployment is close to zero.

16.   A person who has given up searching for work is called:

    a.   frictioinally unemployed.
    b.   structurally unemployed.
    c.   a discouraged worker.
    d.   unemployed.

17.   Sam is a musician who is out of work because electronic equipment replaced live musicians. This is an example of:

    a.   frictional unemployment.
    b.   cyclical unemployment.
    c.   structural unemployment.
    d.   involuntary unemployment.

18.   Consider a broom factory that permanently closes because of foreign competition. If the broom factory's workers cannot find new jobs because their skills are no longer marketable, then they are classified as:

a.   seasonally unemployed.
b.   frictionally unemployed.
c.   structurally unemployed.
d.   cyclically unemployed.

19.   The increase in unemployment associated with a recession is called:

a.   structural unemployment.
b.   frictional unemployment.
c.   discouraged unemployment.
d.   cyclical unemployment.
e.   temporary unemployment.

20.   Which of the following is *true*?

a.   The GDP gap is the difference between full-employment real GDP and actual real GDP.
b.   We desire economic growth because it increases the nation's standard of living.
c.   Economic growth is measured by the annual percentage increase in a nation's real GDP.
d.   Discouraged workers are a reason critics say the unemployment rate is understated.
e.   All of the above are true.

■ TRUE OR FALSE

1.   T   F   Business cycles are recurring periods of economic growth and decline in an economy's real GDP.

2.   T   F   The term "recovery" refers to the maximum point of the business cycle.

3.   T   F   A person who has lost his or her job because it is now performed by a robot is structurally unemployed.

4.   T   F   Structural unemployment refers to short periods of unemployment needed to match jobs and job seekers.

5.   T   F   To be counted as unemployed, a person must be looking for a job.

6.   T   F   The civilian labor force includes only the employed.

7.   T   F   The official unemployment rate can be criticized for both understating and overstating the true number of unemployed.

8.   T   F   When actual real GDP output is below full-employment real GDP, the GDP measures the cost of cyclical unemployment.

■ CROSSWORD PUZZLE

Fill in the crossword puzzle from the list of key concepts. Not all concepts are used.

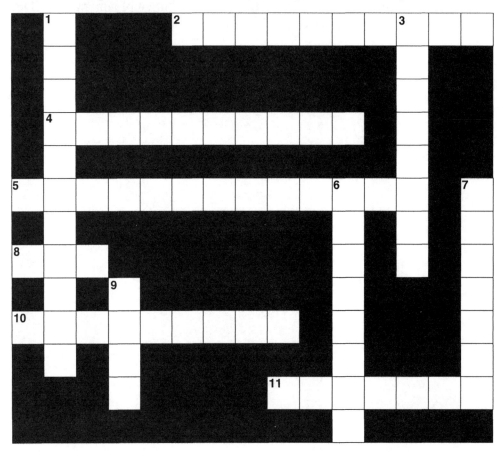

ACROSS

2. _____ unemployment is caused by a mismatch of the skills of workers out of work and the skills required for existing job opportunities.
4. _____ indicators are variables that change at the same time that real GDP changes.
5. Alternating periods of economic growth and contraction.
8. The GDP _____ is the difference between full-employment real GDP and actual real GDP.
10. A downturn in the business cycle.
11. The _____ indicators are variables that change before real GDP changes.

DOWN

1. A _____ worker is a person not counted in the unemployment rate.
3. An upturn in the business cycle.
6. _____ unemployment is caused by the lack of jobs during a recession.
7. _____ indicators are variables that change after real GDP changes.
9. The phase of the business cycle during which real GDP reaches its maximum after rising during a recovery.

■ ANSWERS

Completion Questions

1. business cycle
2. recession
3. economic growth
4. coincident indicators
5. labor force
6. discouraged workers
7. frictional unemployment

8. structural unemployment
9. cyclical unemployment
10. full unemployment
11. GDP gap
12. peak
13. trough
14. recovery

15. leading indicators
16. unemployment rate
17. coincident indicators
18. seasonal unemployment
19. lagging indicators

Multiple Choice

1. e 2. d 3. d 4. e 5. d 6. b 7. c 8. b 9. c 10. d 11. a 12. c 13. b 14. a 15. b 16. c 17. c 18. c 19. d 20. e

True or False

1. True 2. False 3. True 4. False 5. True 6. False 7. True 8. False

Crossword Puzzle

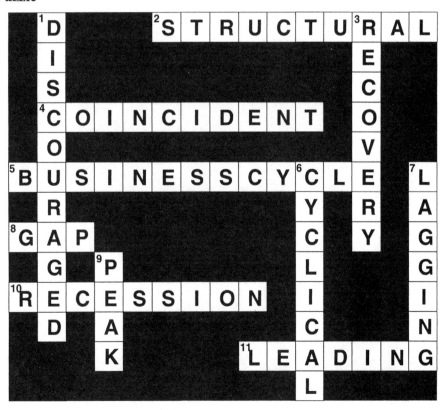

Chapter 7
Inflation

■ CHAPTER IN A NUTSHELL

This chapter explains how inflation is measured and the consequences of inflation. Inflation is a general upward movement in the price level. Changes in the price level are measured by the consumer price index (CPI) published by the Bureau of Labor Statistics. Unlike the GDP deflator, the CPI is based on a "market basket" of items purchased by a typical family. Between 1969 and 1982, the inflation rate averaged 7.6 percent. Since 1983, inflation has moderated and has averaged about 3 percent annually. Inflation can produce a redistribution of income and wealth. Real income adjusts nominal income for inflation. People whose nominal income do not rise faster than the rate of inflation lose purchasing power. Inflation can hurt lenders and savers when the real rate of interest is negative.

The chapter concludes with a discussion of demand-pull and cost-push inflation. Demand-pull occurs at or close to full employment. Cost-push inflation is the result of an increase in the costs of production. Finally, the chapter compares inflation in other countries and discusses the condition of runaway inflation.

■ KEY CONCEPTS

Base year	Inflation
Consumer price index (CPI)	Nominal income
Cost-push inflation	Nominal interest rate
Deflation	Real income
Demand-pull inflation	Real interest rate
Disinflation	Wage-price inflation spiral
Hyperinflation	Wealth

■ MASTER THE LEARNING OBJECTIVES

Please visit the Tucker Xtra! site at http://tuckerxtra.swlearning.com to find the interactive version of the "Master the Learning Objectives" feature.

#1 - Explain how the consumer price index (CPI) and the inflation rate are computed.

Step 1   Read the section in your textbook titled *"Meaning and Measurement of Inflation."*

Step 2   Watch the *CNN Video Clip* titled *"What the Fed Watches"* and analyze how changes in components of the CPI affect the inflation rate.

Step 3   Read the *EconNews* article titled *"Consumers Spend, Prices Rise."* This article describes examples of spending categories for the CPI.

The Result   Following these steps, you have learned that the CPI is based on the average prices of goods and services purchased by a typical family in a base year. The inflation rate is the percentage increase in the CPI between two years.

#2 - Compute the consequences of inflation on nominal income, wealth and the interest rate.

Step 1   Read sections in your textbook titled *"Consequences of Inflation," Demand-Pull and Cost-Push Inflation,"* and *"Inflation in Other Countries."*

Step 2   Listen to the *"Ask the Instructor Video Clip"* titled *"What Are the Principal Functions of Money?"* You will learn of the consequences of hyperinflation.

Step 3   Read the *EconNews* article titled *"Long-Term Trend or Short-Term Jolt?"* This article describes inflation expectations.

The Result   Following these steps, you have learned that people lose purchasing power when their nominal incomes increase less than the rate of inflation. And when the nominal rate of interest adjusted for inflation is negative, lenders and savers lose.

■ COMPLETION QUESTIONS

1.   The _____ measures the cost of purchasing a market basket of goods and services by a typical household during a time period relative to the cost of the same bundle during a base year.

2.   During the early years of the Great Depression, the CPI declined at about a double-digit rate which is called _____.

3.   Between 1980 and 1986 _____ occurred. This does not mean that prices were falling, only that the inflation rate fell.

4.   To measure your purchasing power, requires converting _____ to which adjusts for inflation.

5.   The _____ is the nominal interest rate adjusted for inflation.

6.   _____ is caused by pressure on prices originating from the buyers side of the market. On the other hand, _____ is caused by pressure on price originating from the seller's side of the market.

7.   _____ can cause serious disruptions to an economy by causing inflation psychosis, credit market collapses, a wage-price inflation spiral, and speculation.

8.   _____ occurs when increases in nominal wages cause higher prices and in turn higher wages and prices.

9.   An increase in the general (average) price level of goods and services in the economy is called _____.

10.   The _____ is chosen as a reference point for comparison with some earlier or later year.

11.   The value of the stock of assets owned at some point in time is called_____.

12.   The _____ is the actual rate of interest earned over a period of time.

■ MULTIPLE CHOICE

1.   Inflation is measured by an increase in:

      a.   homes, autos and basic resources.
      b.   prices of all products in the economy.
      c.   the consumer price index (CPI).
      d.   none of the above.

2.   The consumer price index (CPI):

      a.   adjusts for changes in product quality.
      b.   includes separate market baskets of goods and services for both base and current years.
      c.   includes only goods and services bought by the typical urban consumer.
      d.   uses current year quantities of goods and services.

3.   Suppose a market basket of goods and services costs $1,000 in the base year and the consumer price index (CPI) is currently 110. This indicates the price of the market basket of goods and services is now:

      a. $110.
      b. $1,000.
      c. $1,100.
      d. $1,225.

Exhibit 1 Consumer Price Index

Year	Consumer Price Index
1	100
2	110
3	115
4	120
5	125

4.   As shown in Exhibit 1, the rate of inflation for Year 2 is:

a. 5 percent.
b. 10 percent.
c. 20 percent.
d. 25 percent.

5.   As shown in Exhibit 1, the rate of inflation for Year 5 is:

a. 4.2 percent
b. 5 percent.
c. 20 percent.
d. 25 percent.

6.   Disinflation means a decrease in the:

a. general level of prices in the economy.
b. prices of all products in the economy.
c. circular flow.
d. none of the above.

7.   Suppose the price of banana rises over time and consumers respond by buying fewer bananas. This situation contributes to which bias in the consumer price index?

a. Substitution bias.
b. Transportation bias.
c. Quality bias.
d. Indexing bias.

8.   Which of the following is *correct*?

a.   The percentage change in real income equals the percentage change in nominal income plus the percentage change in CPI.
b.   Real income equals nominal income multiplied by the CPI as a decimal.
c.   People whose nominal incomes rise faster than the rate of inflation lose purchasing power.
d.   All of the above.
e.   None of the above.

9.   Real income in 2000 is equal to:

a.   2000 nominal income x CPI.
b. $\frac{2000\ nominal\ income}{2000\ real\ output}$ x 100.
c. $\frac{2000\ nominal\ income}{2000\ real\ GDP}$ x 100.
d.   none of the above.

10.   If the rate of inflation in a given time period turns out to be higher than lenders and borrowers anticipated, then the effect will be:

a.   a redistribution of wealth from borrowers to lenders.
b.   a net gain in purchasing power for lenders relative to borrowers.
c.   no change in the distribution of wealth between lenders and borrowers.
d.   none of the above.

11.   Demand–pull inflation occurs:

a.   when "too much money is chasing too many goods."
b.   because of excess factor payments.
c.   at or close to a recession.
d.   all of the above.
e.   none of the above.

12.   Cost–push inflation is due to:

a.   "too much money chasing too few goods."
b.   the economy operating at full employment.
c.   increases in production costs.
d.   all of the above.

13.   Suppose that your income during 1999 was $50,000, and the CPI for 1999 was 150 (base year = 1992). Back in 1992 your income was $30,000. Has your real income increased or decreased from 1992 to 1999? By how much?

   a.   Increased by $5,000.
   b.   Increased by $3,333.33.
   c.   Unchanged.
   d.   Decreased by $3,333.33
   e.   Decreased by $5,000.

14.   If the bank offers you a nominal interest rate of 9 percent on a student loan, and if inflation is 6 percent, then what is the real interest rate?

   a.   15 percent.
   b.   9 percent.
   c.   6 percent.
   d.   3 percent.

15.   Consider borrowers and lenders who agree to loans with fixed nominal interest rates. If inflation is higher than what the borrowers and lenders expected, then who benefits from lower real interest rates?

   a.   Only the borrowers benefit.
   b.   Only the lenders benefit.
   c.   Both borrowers and lenders benefit.
   d.   Neither borrowers nor lenders.

16.   One way the consumer price index (CPI) differs from the GDP chain price index is that the CPI:

   a.   uses current year quantities of goods and services.
   b.   includes separate market baskets of goods and services for both base and current years.
   c.   includes only goods and services bought by typical urban consumers.
   d.   is bias free.

17. As the price of gasoline rose during the 1970s, consumers cut back on their use of gasoline relative to other consumer goods. This situation contributed to which bias in the consumer price index?

   a. Substitution bias.
   b. Trasportation bias.
   c. Quality bias.
   d. Indexing bias.

18. If the inflation rate exceeds the nominal rate of interest,

   a. the real interest rate is negative.
   b. lenders lose.
   c. savers lose.
   d. all of the above.

19. Suppose you place $10,000 in a retirement fund that earns a nominal interest rate of 8 percent. If you expect inflation to be 5 percent or lower, then you are expecting to earn a real interest rate of at least:

   a. 1.6 percent.
   b. 3 percent.
   c. 4 percent.
   d. 5 percent.

20. During the 1970s, the Organization of Petroleum Exporting Countries (OPEC) sharply increased the price of oil, which triggered higher inflation rates in the United States. This type of inflation is *best* classified as:

   a. pseudo-inflation.
   b. demand-pull inflation.
   c. cost-push inflation.
   d. hyperinflation.

■ TRUE OR FALSE

1. T   F   Inflation occurs when there is an increase in the purchasing power of money.

2. T   F   Unlike the GDP deflator, the CPI does not consider goods and services purchased by business and government.

3. T   F   Disinflation and deflation mean a decrease in the average price level.

4.   T   F   A consumer price index of 110 for a given year indicates that prices in that year are 10 percent higher than prices in the base year.

5.   T   F   If it costs $240 in 2003 to buy the same market basket of goods that costs $120 in the base year of 1985, a consumer price index (CPI) for 2003, would have a value of 200.

6.   T   F   If consumers reduce the purchase of goods whose relative prices rise (substitute bias), the consumer price index will tend to have an upward bias over time.

7.   T   F   Changes in the quality of some goods and services, such as electromechanical calculators, are thought to give a downward bias to the consumer price index.

8.   T   F   People with fixed incomes tend to fare best in an inflationary period.

9.   T   F   Demand–pull inflationary pressure increases as the economy approaches full employment.

10.   T   F   Cost–push inflation is caused by too much money chasing too few goods.

■ CROSSWORD PUZZLE

Fill in the crossword puzzle from the list of key concepts. Not all of the concepts are used.

ACROSS

1. The value of assets.
3. The _____ is an index that measures changes in the average prices of consumer goods and services.
6. _____ inflation is a rise in the price level caused by total spending.
8. A reduction in the rate of inflation.
9. A decrease in the average price level.
10. A _____ spiral is a situation that occurs when increases in nominal wage rates are passed on in higher prices, which, in turn, result in even higher nominal wage rates and prices.
11. _____ income is the actual dollars received over a period of time.

DOWN

2. An extremely rapid rise in the price level.
4. An increase in the average price level.
5. Income adjusted for inflation.
7. A year chosen as a reference point.

■ ANSWERS

Completion Questions

1. consumer price index (CPI)
2. deflation
3. disinflation
4. nominal income, real income
5. real interest rate
6. demand–pull inflation, cost–push inflation
7. hyperinflation
8. wage–price spiral
9. inflation
10. base year
11. wealth
12. nominal interest rate

Multiple Choice

1. c 2. c 3. c 4. b 5. a 6. d 7. a 8. e 9. d 10. d 11. e 12. c 13. b 14. d 15. a 16. c 17. a 18. d 19. b 20. c

True or False

1. False 2. True 3. False 4. True 5. True 6. True 7. False 8. False 9. True 10. False

Crossword Puzzle

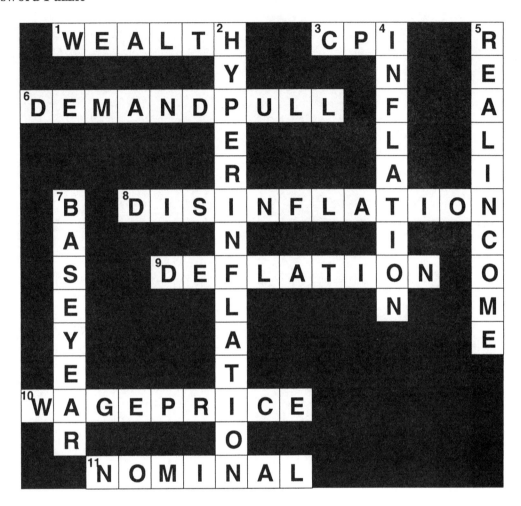

Chapter 8
The Keynesian Model

■ CHAPTER IN A NUTSHELL

The classical theory relied on Say's law which states "supply creates its own demand." To the classical economists capitalism would guarantee an equilibrium (or stable) level of economic activity at full employment. Flexible wages, prices, and interest rates would ensure this.

Keynes rejected the classical notion of Say's law. He argued that underspending was very likely. Keynes focused on aggregate demand (total spending) as being the key determinant to the level of macroeconomic activity. Aggregate demand (or total spending) equals the sum of consumption, investment, government and net export spending. This chapter focuses on consumption and investment spending (expenditures).

Consumption spending is directly related to real disposable income and is expressed as an upward-sloping consumption function. As income rises, consumption spending rises. The marginal propensity to consume (MPC) equals the slope of the consumption function. If there is a change in a nonincome determinant, such as expectations, wealth, the price level, the interest rate, or the stock of durable goods, this causes a shift of the consumption function.

The investment demand curve represents the inverse relationship between the interest rate and the level of investment spending. The investment demand curve can shift if there is a change in expectations, technology, capacity utilization, or business taxes. If we assume investment spending is independent of the level of income, the investment function is graphically expressed as a horizontal line at a dollar amount of investment spending determined by those nonincome variables just mentioned above.

When we add consumption and investment spending schedules (functions) together, we get the aggregate expenditures (total spending) function (there is no government spending, exports or imports in the economy-we haven't considered them yet).

■ KEY CONCEPTS

Aggregate expenditures function	Investment demand curve
Autonomous expenditure	Marginal propensity to consume (MPC)
Autonomous consumption	Marginal propensity to save (MPS)
Classical economists	Saving
Consumption function	Say's Law
Dissaving	

■ MASTER THE LEARNING OBJECTIVES

Please visit the Tucker Xtra! site at http://tuckerxtra.swlearning.com to find the interactive version of the "Master the Learning Objectives" feature.

#1 - Define the consumption function.

Step 1   Read the sections in your textbook titled *"Introducing Classical Theory and the Keynesian Revolution"* and *"Reasons the Consumption Function Shifts."*

Step 2   Watch the Graphing Workshop *"See It!"* tutorial titled *"Consumption Function."* Study how this concept is computed.

Step 3   Read the Graphing Workshop *"Grasp It!"* exercise titled *"Consumption Function."* This exercise uses a slider bar to demonstrate how changes in real disposable income and the marginal propensity to consume (MPC) affect the consumption function.

Step 4   Create a new graph at the Graphing Workshop *"Try It!"* titled *"Consumption Function."* This exercise illustrates how a consumption function is derived.

Step 5   Play the *"Causation Chains Game"* titled *"Movement Along and Shifts in the Consumption Function."*

Step 6   Listen to the *"Ask the Instructor Video Clip"* titled *"Can We Make Sense Out of the Consumption Function?"* You will learn the relationship between the marginal propensity to consume (MPC) and the consumption function (C).

Step 7   Read the *EconNews* titled *"It's Suppose to be a Two-Edged Sword."* This article describes the wealth effect.

Step 8   Read the *EconNews* titled *"The Pauper Effect."* This article describes the impact of the wealth effect.

The Result   Following these steps, you have learned that a consumption function is the relationship between disposable income and consumption, and the MPC is the slope of the consumption function (the change in consumption as income changes).

#2 - Explain the investment, demand curve and its relationship to the aggregate expenditures function.

Step 1   Read the sections in your textbook titled *"Investment Expenditures," "Why Investment Demand is Unstable,"* and *"The Aggregate Expenditures Function."*

Step 2   Read the Graphing Workshop *"Grasp It!"* exercise titled *"Keynesian Cross."* This exercise uses a slider bar to demonstrate how changes in autonomous spending affect the aggregate expenditures curve.

Step 3   Play the *"Causation Chains Game"* titled *"Movement Along and Shifts in a Firm's Investment Demand."*

The Result   Following these steps, you have learned that a firm's investment curve depends on the interest rate and profit expectations for each potential investment expenditures. You have also derived an aggregate expenditure function constructed with autonomous expenditure and the investment demand curve.

#3 - Examine how a stock market crash affects the economy.

Step 1   Read the *"You're the Economist"* in your textbook titled *"Does a Stock Market Crash Affect the Economy."*

Step 2   Listen to the *"Ask the Instructor Video Clip"* titled *"How Would a Stock Market Crash Affect the Economy?"* You will learn how a downturn in the stock market affects components of GDP spending.

Step 3   Read the *EconNews* titled *"Consumer Confidence Crisis."* This article describes the relationship between the stock market and The Consumer Confidence Index.

The Result   Following these steps, you have learned that a stock market crash attracts media attention and can decrease the consumption (C) and investment (I) components of GDP.

THE ECONOMIST'S TOOL KIT
Developing the Keynesian Aggregate Expenditures Function

Error! Bookmark not defined.*Step one:* Begin by drawing a 45 degree line. Along this line consumption (C) equals disposable income (Y_d). Draw a consumption function (C). At the break-even income, saving is zero. The slope of C is the marginal propensity to consume (MPC) which is the ratio of ΔC to ΔY_d.

Step two: A movement along the consumption function C_1 is caused by a change in Y_d. An upward shift to C_2 is caused by a change in a nonincome determinant that increases autonomous consumption from a_1 to a_2.

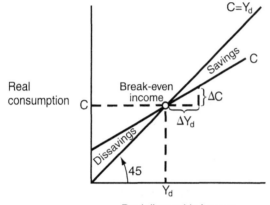

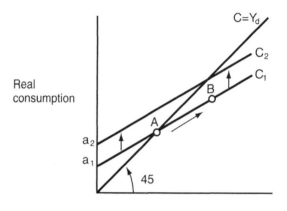

Step three: Assume that autonomous real investment expenditures are independent of the level of real disposable income per year. This means the investment curve (I) is a straight line with zero slope.

Step four: The Keynesian aggregate expenditures function (AE) begins with the consumption function (C). Next, the investment demand curve (I) is added to obtain the AE function (C + I). The vertical distance between AE and C is equal to the level of autonomous investment (I).

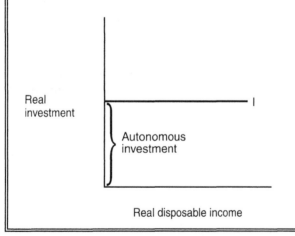

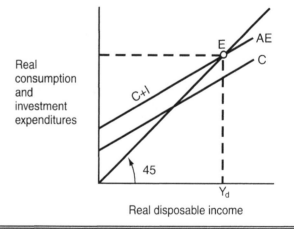

■ COMPLETION QUESTIONS

1. _____ is the theory that supply creates its own demand.

2. The graph that shows the amount households spend for goods and service at different levels of disposable income is called _____.

3. _____ is the amount by which personal consumption expenditures exceed disposable income.

4. _____ is consumption that is independent of the level of disposable income.

5. The part of disposable income households do not spend for consumer goods and services is called _____.

6. _____ is the change in consumption resulting from a given change in real disposable income.

7. _____ is the change in saving resulting from a given change in real disposable income.

8. The curve that shows the amount businesses spend for investment goods at different possible rates of interest is called the _____.

9. Spending that does not vary with the current level of disposable income is called _____.

10. The _____ represents total spending in an economy at a given level of real disposable income.

11. A group of economists who believed recessions would naturally be eliminated by the price system is called _____.

■ MULTIPLE CHOICE

1. Classical economic theory predicted that in the long run the economy would experience:

    a. idle factors of production.
    b. rising rate of inflation.
    c. below full employment.
    d. full employment.

2.   The relationship between consumer expenditures and disposable income is the:

   a.   savings function.
   b.   the tax rate function.
   c.   disposable income function.
   d.   consumption function.

3.   Autonomous consumption is equal to the level of consumption associated with:

   a.   unstable disposable income.
   b.   positive disposable income.
   c.   zero disposable income.
   d.   negative disposable income.

4.   The marginal propensity to consume (MPC) is computed as the change in consumption divided by the change in:

   a.   GDP.
   b.   disposable personal income.
   c.   saving.
   d.   none of the above.

5.   If your disposable personal income increases from $40,000 to $48,000 and your consumption increases from $35,000 to $39,000, your marginal propensity to consume (MPC) is:

   a.   0.2.
   b.   0.4.
   c.   0.5.
   d.   0.8.
   e.   1.0.

Exhibit 1 Consumption function

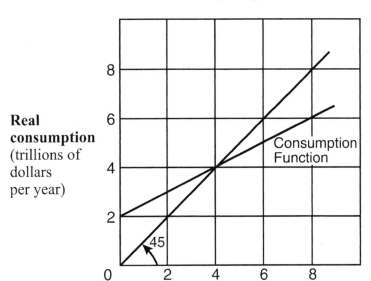

6.   As shown in Exhibit 1, autonomous consumption is:

a.   0.
b. $2 trillion.
c. $4 trillion.
d. $6 trillion.
e. $8 trillion.

7.   As shown in Exhibit 1, saving occurs:

a.   at 0 disposable income.
b.   between $0 and $4 trillion disposable income.
c.   at $4 trillion disposable income.
d.   at a disposable income greater than $4 trillion.

8.   As shown in Exhibit 1, the marginal propensity to consumer (MPC) is:

a.   0.25.
b.   0.50.
c.   0.75.
d.   0.90.

9.   As shown in Exhibit 1, the marginal propensity to save (MPS) is:

   a.   0.25.
   b.   0.50.
   c.   0.75.
   d.   0.90.

10.   A movement along in the consumption function is caused by a change in:

   a.   real GDP.
   b.   can be caused by a change in the price level.
   c.   the marginal propensity to consume (MPC).
   d.   None of the above.

11.   Which of the following would shift the investment demand curve rightward?

   a.   Firms are operating their plants at less than full capacity.
   b.   A decrease in the interest rate.
   c.   A decrease in business taxes.
   d.   All of the above.
   e.   None of the above.

Exhibit 2 Aggregate expenditures function

Real disposable income
(trillions of dollars per year)

12.   As shown in Exhibit 2, autonomous consumption is:

    a.   0.
    b. $2 trillion.
    c. $4 trillion.
    d. $6 trillion.
    e. $8 trillion.

13.   As shown in Exhibit 2, the marginal propensity to consume (MPC) is:

    a.   0.33.
    b.   0.50.
    c.   0.67.
    d.   0.75.

14.   As shown in Exhibit 2, this economy is in macro equilibrium at:

    a. $8 trillion.
    b. $12 trillion.
    c. $16 trillion.
    d.   None of the above.

15.   Which of the following correctly describes the marginal propensity to consume?

    a.   The change in savings divided by the change in consumption.
    b.   The change in consumption divided by the change in real disposable income.
    c.   The change in real disposable income divided by the change in consumption.
    d.   The change in savings divided by the change in real disposable income.

16.   If the marginal propensity to consume is 0.80, then what is the marginal propensity to save?

    a.   -0.80.
    b.   0.00.
    c.   0.20.
    d.   0.80.
    e.   1.00

17.   Which of the following will most likely cause an outward shift in a firm's investment demand?

   a.   A decrease in interest rates.
   b.   Low levels of existing capacity utilization.
   c.   Expectations of higher future business profitability.
   d.   An increase in interest rates.

18.   The French economist Jean-Baptiste Say transformed the equality of total output and total spending into a law that can be expressed as follows:

   a.   Unemployment is not possible in the short run.
   b.   Demand and supply are never equal.
   c.   Supply creates its own demand.
   d.   Demand creates its own supply.

19.   What is the title of the John Marnard Keynes's book published in 1936 that challenged the classical self-correction economic theory?

   a.   *In the Long-run We Are Dead.*
   b.   *Classical Economics Revised.*
   c.   *General Theory of Employment, Interest, and Money.*
   d.   *A Keynesian Approach to Economic Policy.*

20.   Which of the following will shift the consumption function upward?

   a.   An increase in consumer wealth.
   b.   An increase in the interest rate.
   c.   An increase in personal income taxes.
   d.   A decrease in the MPC.
   e.   An increase in disposable income.

■ TRUE OR FALSE

1.   T   F   The consumption function has a positive slope.

2.   T   F   If autonomous consumption is greater than zero and the marginal propensity to consume is greater than zero, but less than one, the consumption function will first be below and then above the 45 degree line.

3.   T   F   Saving is the portion of disposable personal income *not* spent on investment.

4.   T   F   The marginal propensity to consume (MPC) is the change in consumption divided by the change in saving.

5.   T   F   If people become pessimistic about the state of the economy, the consumption function shifts upward.

6.   T   F   An increase in consumer wealth shifts the consumption function upward.

7.   T   F   Real investment spending for the past 35 years is more volatile than real personal consumption.

8.   T   F   If firms increase investment, the aggregate expenditures function will shift downward, other things being equal.

■ CROSSWORD PUZZLE

Fill in the crossword puzzle from the list of key concepts. Not all of the concepts are used.

ACROSS

2.   _____ expenditures are spending that does not vary with the current level of disposable income.

3.   _____ demand curve is the curve that shows the amount businesses spend for investment goods at different possible rates of interest.

6.   The theory that supply creates its own demand.

8.   The marginal propensity to _____ is the change in consumption resulting from a given change in real disposable income.

DOWN

1.   _____ function is the graph that shows the amount households spend for goods and services at different levels of disposable income.

4.   _____ is the change in saving resulting from a given change in real disposable income.

6.   _____ is the part of disposable income households do not spend for consumer goods and services.

7.   The _____ expenditures function is the function that represents total spending in an economy at a given level of real disposable income.

ANSWERS

Completion Questions

1. Say's Law
2. consumption function
3. dissaving
4. autonomous consumption
5. saving
6. marginal propensity to consume (MPC)
7. marginal propensity to save (MPS)
8. investment demand curve
9. autonomous expenditure
10. aggregate expenditures function (AE)
11. classical economists

Multiple Choice

1. d 2. d 3. c 4. b 5. c 6. b 7. d 8. b 9. b 10. a 11. c 12. c 13. b 14. b 15. b 16. c 17. c 18. c 19. c 20. a

True or False

1. True 2. False 3. False 4. False 5. False 6. True 7. True 8. False

Crossword Puzzle

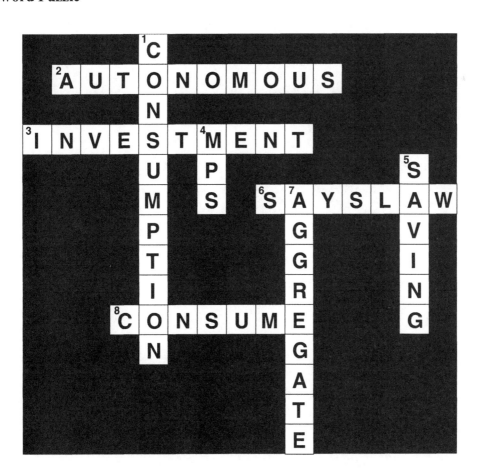

Chapter 9
The Keynesian Model in Action

■ CHAPTER IN A NUTSHELL

This chapter builds on the last by adding government spending and net exports to the aggregate expenditures (total spending) function to determine the equilibrium level of economy activity. Both government spending and net exports are treated as autonomous spending components in aggregate expenditures. Government spending is largely determined by political forces. Net exports (exports minus imports) are determined by foreign and domestic income, tastes, trade restrictions, and exchange rates.

The Keynesian aggregate expenditures-output model determines the equilibrium level of real GDP graphically by the intersection of the aggregate expenditures and the aggregate output and income schedules. At any other output-income level unintended inventory investment pressures businesses to alter aggregate output and income until equilibrium is restored. However, equilibrium does not necessarily achieve full employment.

Changes in any of the components of total spending will cause a multiplier effect on the equilibrium level of output and income. The change in the income-output level is determined by multiplying the initial change in total spending. The multiplier equals the reciprocal of the MPS. The multiplier effect causes any initial change in aggregate expenditures to result in a much larger in the income-output level.

Because equilibrium is not necessarily at full employment, a recessionary or inflationary gap is possible. A recessionary (inflationary) gap measures the amount by which total spending falls short of (is greater than) the required amout to achieve full employment. In the Keynesian model, changes in government spending and taxes can close a recessionary or inflationary gap. By doing so, government can moderate the problems of cyclical unemployment and slow growth experienced during a recession, and demand-pull inflation experienced during an expansionary phase of the business cycle.

■ KEY CONCEPTS

Aggregate expenditures-output model
Inflationary gap
Recessionary gap
Tax multiplier
Spending multiplier

■ MASTER THE LEARNING OBJECTIVES

Please visit the Tucker Xtra! site at http://tuckerxtra.swlearning.com to find the interactive version of the "Master the Learning Objectives" feature.

#1 - Understand that the aggregate expenditures-output model determines equilibrium real GDP.

Step 1   Read the sections in your textbook titled *"Adding Government and International Trade to the Keynesian Model,"* and *"The Aggregate Expenditures-Output Model."*

Step 2   Watch the Graphing Workshop *"See It!"* tutorial titled *"Keynesian Cross."* Study how equilibrium real GDP is established by inventory accumulation and depletion.

Step 3   Create a new graph at the Graphing Workshop *"Try It!"* titled *"Keyneisan Cross."* This exercise illustrates the construction of the aggregate expenditures output model (Keynesian Cross).

The Result   Following these steps, you have learned to construct the complete aggregate expenditures-output model including consumption (C), investment (I), government spending (G), and net exports (X - M).

#2 - Interpret the ability of the spending multiplier effect to combat recession or inflation.

Step 1   Read the section in your textbook *"The Spending Multiplier Effect."*

Step 2   Play the *"Causation Chains Game"* titled *"The Multiplier Effect and Government Spending."*

Step 3   Listen to the *"Ask the Instructor Video Clip"* titled *"What Do Economists Mean by the Term 'Multiplier'?"* You will learn the common sense meaning of the spending multiplier and how it is computed based on the marginal propensity to consume (MPC).

Step 4   Listen to the *"Ask the Instructor Video Clip"* titled *"Does the Multiplier Work in Both Directions?"* You will learn how the spending multiplier operates to increase or decrease real GDP.

Step 5   Listen to the *"Ask the Instructor Video Clip"* titled *"In Theory How Does a Tax Cut Work to Stimulate the Economy?"* You will learn the theory of the Keynesian tax multiplier and discuss the President Bush tax cut.

The Result   Following these steps, you have learned that an initial change in spending creates a chain reaction of further spending that causes a greater cumulative change in real GDP. Given the value of the multiplier and the difference between actual and full-employment real GDP (GDP gap), the government can increase or decrease spending to eliminate the GDP gap.

THE ECONOMIST'S TOOL KIT
Using the Keynesian Model to Achieve Full Employment

Step one: Below the equilibrium real GDP (Y^*), inventory depletion causes businesses to increase production and the economy expands toward Y^*.

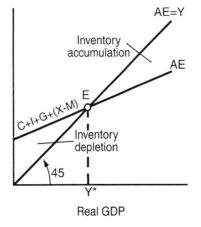

Step two: From equilibrium at point E_1, assume the government increases spending (ΔG). The AE_1 line shifts vertically upward to AE_2 and equilibrium changes from E_1 to E_2. Thus, the multiplier process has caused real GDP to increase from Y_1^* to Y_2^*.

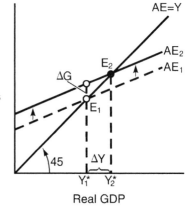

Step three: Begin in equilibrium at E_1 which means Y_1^* is below full employment at Y_2^*. The vertical distance between E_2 and point a measures the increase in aggregate spending necessary to achieve full employment (recessionary gap).

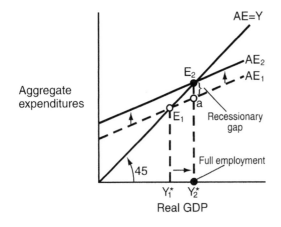

Step four: Here the economy is in equilibrium at E_1 with Y_1^* above the full-employment real GDP of Y_2^*. The vertical distance between points a and E_2 measures the decrease in aggregate spending necessary to achieve full employment (inflationary gap).

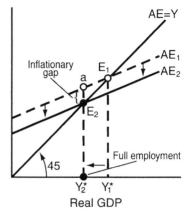

■ COMPLETION QUESTIONS

1.   The _____ determines the equilibrium level of real GDP by the intersection of the   aggregate expenditures and aggregate output (and income) curves.

2.   The ratio of the change in real GDP to the initial change in any component of aggregate expenditures, including consumption, investment, government purchases, and net exports is called _____.

3.   A _____ is the amount by which aggregate expenditures fall short of the amount required to achieve full-employment equilibrium.

4.   The amount by which aggregate expenditures exceed the amount required to achieve full-employment equilibrium is called _____.

5.   A _____ is the change in aggregate expenditure (total spending) resulting from an initial change in taxes.

■ MULTIPLE CHOICE

1.   Using C to represent consumption, I to represent investment, G to represent government spending, S to represent saving, X to represent exports, and M to represent imports, aggregate expenditures can be represented by:

   a.   C + I + G + (X-M) - S.
   b.   (C -S) + G + (X-M).
   c.   C + I + G + (X + M).
   d.   none of the above.

2.   In the aggregate expenditures-output model, if aggregate expenditures (AE) are greater than GDP, then:

   a.   employment decreases.
   b.   inventory is accumulated.
   c.   inventory is unchanged.
   d.   inventory is depleted.

3.   In the aggregate expenditures-output model, if an economy operates above equilibrium GDP, there will be:

    a.   unplanned inventory accumulation.
    b.   a decrease in GDP.
    c.   a decrease in employment.
    d.   none of the above.
    e.   all of the above.

Exhibit 1   Keynesian aggregate-expenditures model

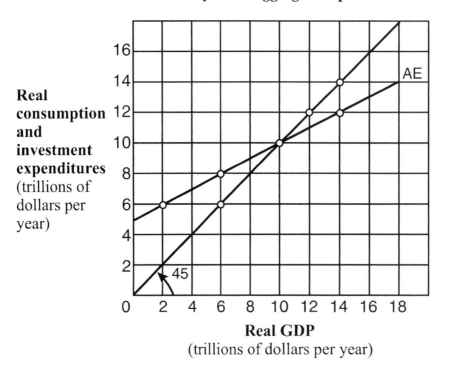

4.   As shown in Exhibit 1, equilibrium GDP is:

    a. $2 trillion.
    b. $6 trillion.
    c. $10 trillion.
    d. $12 trillion.
    e. $14 trillion.

5.   As shown in Exhibit 1, if GDP is $6 trillion, the economy experiences unplanned inventory:

    a.   depletion of $2 trillion.
    b.   depletion of $6 trillion.
    c.   accumulation of $2 trillion.
    d.   accumulation of $6 trillion.
    e.   none of the above.

6.   As shown in Exhibit 1, if GDP is $14 trillion, the economy experiences unplanned inventory:

    a.   accumulation of $12 trillion.
    b.   depletion of $14 trillion.
    c.   accumulation of $2 trillion.
    d.   depletion of $4 trillion.

7.   The formula to compute the spending multiplier is:

    a. $1/(C + I)$.
    b. $1/(1 - MPS)$.
    c. $1/(MPC + MPS)$.
    d.   none of the above.

8.   If the marginal propensity to consume (MPC) is 0.80, the value of the spending multiplier is:

    a.   2.
    b.   5.
    c.   8.
    d.   10.

9.   If the marginal propensity to save (MPS) is 0.25, the value of the spending multiplier is:

    a.   1.
    b.   2.
    c.   4.
    d.   9.

10.   Which of the following options could be used to eliminate a recessionary gap?

    a.   Decrease government spending.
    b.   Decrease consumption.
    c.   Decrease investment.
    d.   Decrease transfer payments.
    e.   None of the above.

11.   In the aggregate expenditures-output model, a tax increase causes a (an):

    a.   upward shift in the aggregate expenditures curve.
    b.   downward shift in the aggregate expenditures curve.
    c.   shift in the 45-degree line.
    d.   rightward movement along the aggregate expenditures curve.
    e.   leftward movement along the aggregate expenditures curve.

12.   Use the aggregate expenditures-output model and assume an economy is in equilibrium at \$5 trillion which is \$250 billion below full-employment GDP. If the marginal propensity to consume (MPC) is 0.60, full-employment GDP can be reached if government spending:

    a.   increases by \$60 billion.
    b.   increases by \$250 billion.
    c.   is held constant.
    d.   none of the above.

13.   Using the aggregate expenditure-output model, assume the aggregate expenditures (AE) line is above the 45-degree line at full-employment GDP. This vertical distance is called a (an):

    a.   inflationary gap.
    b.   recessionary gap.
    c.   negative GDP gap.
    d.   marginal propensity to consume gap.

14.   Use the aggregate expenditures-output model and assume the marginal propensity to consume (MPC) is 0.80. A decrease in government spending of $1 billion would result in a decrease in GDP of:

a. $0.
b. $0.8 billion.
c. $1.0 billion.
d. $8.0 billion.
e.   none of the above.

15.   Use the aggregate expenditures-output model and assume an economy is in equilibrium at $6 trillion which is $500 billion above full-employment GDP. If the marginal propensity to consume (MPC) is 0.75, full-employment GDP can be reached if government spending:

a.   decreases by $75 billion.
b.   decreases by $500 billion.
c.   is held constant.
d.   none of the above.

16.   If the equilibrium level of real GDP is $100,000 below the full employment level of real GDP and the spending multiplier is 4, how much of an increase in autonomous aggregate expenditures (such as government spending) is required to move the equilibrium to the full-employment level of real GDP?

a. $400,000.
b. $200,000.
c. $100,000.
d. $25,000.
e. $10,000.

17.   If the equilibrium level of real GDP is $400,000 above the full employment level of real GDP and the spending multiplier is 4, how much of a decrease in autonomous aggregate expenditures (such as government spending) is required to move the equilibrium down to the full-employment level of real GDP?

a. $400,000.
b. $200,000.
c. $100,000.
d. $25,000.
e. $10,000.

18. If the marginal propensity to consume (MPC) shrinks, then which of the following is *true?*

    a. It takes the same increase in autonomous aggregate expenditures to shift equilibrium real GDP upward to the full-employment level.
    b. It takes a smaller decrease in autonomous aggregate expenditures to shift equilibrium real GDP downward to the full-employment level.
    c. It takes a larger increase in autonomous aggregate expenditures to shift equilibrium real GDP upward to the full-employment level.
    d. It takes the same decrease in autonomous aggregate expenditures to shift equilibrium real GDP downward to the full-employment level.

19. In the aggregate expenditures-output model, an increase in government spending causes a(n):

    a. upward shift in the aggregate expenditures curve.
    b. downward shift in the aggregate expenditures curve.
    c. shift in the 45-degree line.
    d. rightward movement along the aggregate expenditures curve.
    e. leftward movement along the aggregate expenditures curve.

20. The equilibrium level of real GDP is $1,000 billion, the target full-employment level of real GDP is $,1500 billion, and the marginal propensity to consume is 0.75. The target can be reached if government spending is:

    a. increased by $100 billion.
    b. increased by $125 billion.
    c. increased by $50 billion.
    d. held constant.

■ TRUE OR FALSE

1. T   F   In the aggregate expenditures-output model, if aggregate expenditures (AE) are less than GDP, then GDP decreases.

2. T   F   In the aggregate expenditures-output model, if an economy operates below equilibrium GDP, there will be unplanned inventory accumulation.

3. T   F   In the aggregate expenditures-output model, if aggregate expenditures (AE) equals $7 trillion and GDP equals $8 trillion, then inventory depletion equals $1 trillion.

4.   T   F   The spending multiplier effect is the result of a movement along the aggregate expenditures (AE) line.

5.   T   F   The spending multiplier also applies to investment spending by businesses.

6.   T   F   If the marginal propensity to consume is 0.80, the value of the spending multiplier will be 4.

7.   T   F   The size of the spending multiplier depends on the level of real GDP.

8.   T   F   An increase in the marginal propensity to consume (MPC) leads to a increase in the spending multiplier.

9.   T   F   Increasing transfer payments is one option to eliminate an inflationary gap.

10.   T   F   Decreasing transfer payments is one option to eliminate a recessionary gap.

■ CROSSWORD PUZZLE

Fill in the crossword puzzle from the list of key concepts. Not all the concepts are used.

ACROSS

2.   The amount by which aggregate expenditures exceed the amount required to achieve full-employment equilibrium.

3.   The amount by which aggregate expenditures fall short of the amount required to achieve full-employment equilibrium.

4.   The _____ expenditures-output model determines the equilibrium level of real GDP by the intersection of the aggregate expenditures and aggregate output (and income) curves.

DOWN

1.   The spending _____ is the ratio of the change in real GDP to the initial change in any component of aggregate expenditures.

■ ANSWERS

Completion Questions

1. aggregate expenditures-output model
2. spending multiplier
3. recessionary gap
4. inflationary gap
5. tax multiplier

Multiple Choice

1. d 2. d 3. e 4. c 5. a 6. c 7. d 8. b 9. c 10. e 11. b 12. d 13. a 14. e 15. d 16. d 17. c 18. c 19. a 20. b

True or False

1. True 2. False 3. False 4. False 5. True 6. False 7. False 8. True 9. False 10. False

Crossword Puzzle

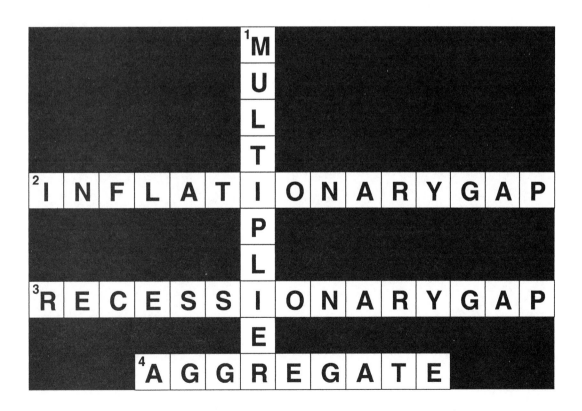

Chapter 10
Aggregate Demand and Supply

■ CHAPTER IN A NUTSHELL

The purpose of this chapter is to explain how the aggregate demand and aggregate supply curves determine the price level and the level of real GDP. The aggregate demand curve slopes downward because of the real balances effect, interest-rate effect, and net exports effect. As explained in chapter on GDP, determinates of the aggregate demand curve are consumption (C), investment (I), government purchases (G), and net exports (X-M). The aggregate supply curve slopes upward and consists of three ranges: Keynesian (horizontal segment), intermediate (rising segment), and classical (vertical segment). The equilibrium level of real GDP and the equilibrium price level are determined by the intersection of the aggregate demand and supply curves. The chapter ends by applying the aggregate demand and supply model to the concepts of demand-pull inflation and cost push inflation introduced in the previous chapter. For example, the text explains how a leftward shift in the aggregate supply curve caused by higher oil prices (cost-push inflation scenario) resulted in stagflation.

■ KEY CONCEPTS

Aggregate demand curve   Keynesian range
Aggregate supply curve   Net exports effect
Classical range   Real balances or wealth effect
Interest-rate effect   Stagflation
Intermediate range

■ MASTER THE LEARNING OBJECTIVES

Please visit the Tucker Xtra! site at http://tuckerxtra.swlearning.com to find the interactive version of the "Master the Learning Objectives" feature.

#1 - Understand aggregate demand curve theory.

Step 1   Read the sections in your textbook titled *"Aggregate Demand Curve," "Reasons for the Aggregate Demand Curve's Shape,"* and *"Nonprice-Level Determinants of Aggregate Demand."*

Step 2   Watch the Graphing Workshop *"See It!"* tutorial titled *"Aggregate Demand."* Study how the aggregate demand curve is derived.

Step 3   Play the *"Causation Chains Game"* titled *"The Aggregate Demand Curve."*

Step 4   Play the *"Causation Chains Game"* titled *"A Shift in the Aggregate Demand Curve."*

Step 5   Read the *EconNews* article titled *"An Easy Christmas Present."* This article describes the primary determinants of aggregate demand.

The Result   Following these steps, you have learned that the aggregate demand curve is downward-sloping and that changes in the price level (CPI) cause movements along the AD curve. Any factor that changes consumption (C), investment spending (I), government spending (G), or net exports (X - M) shifts the AD curve.

2 - Understand aggregate supply curve theory and changes in macroeconomic equilibrium.

Step 1   Read the sections in your textbook titled *"Three Ranges of the Aggregate Supply Curve," "Changes in the AD-AS Macroeconomics Equilibrium,"* and *"Nonprice-Level Determinants of Aggregate Supply."*

Step 2   Read the Graphing Workshop *"Grasp It!"* exercise titled *"Aggregate Demand"* and *"Changes in Aggregate Demand."* These exercises use a slider bar to demonstrate how changes in aggregate demand and supply curves change the price level and level of real GDP.

Step 3   Create new graphs at the Graphing Workshop *"Try It!"* titled *"Aggregate Demand."* This exercise illustrates the impact of increased government spending on macro equilibrium.

Step 4   Play the *"Causation Chains Game"* titled *"The Keynesian Horizontal Aggregate Supply Curve."*

Step 5   Play the *"Causation Chains Game"* titled *"The Classical Vertical Aggregate Supply Curve."*

Step 6   Play the *"Causation Chains Game"* titled *"A Rightward Shift in the Aggregate Supply Curve."*

Step 7   Listen to the *Ask the Instructor Video Clip"* titled *"Can the Aggregate Supply Curve Take on Different Shapes?"* You will learn the conditions that determine the three ranges of the aggregate supply curve.

Step 8   Listen to the *Ask the Instructor Video Clip"* titled *"What Circumstances Can Shift the Aggregate Supply?"* You will learn factors that can increase or decrease the aggregate supply curve.

The Result   Following these steps, you have learned the aggregate supply curve has three ranges: (1) Keynesian range, (2) intermediate range, and (3) classical range. Changes in aggregate demand along these three ranges have various effects on the price level, real GDP, and the unemployment rate.

#3 - Distinguish between cost-push and demand-pull inflation.

Step 1   Read the section in your textbook titled *"Cost-Push and Demand-Pull Inflation Revisited."*

Step 2   Create a new graph at the Graphing Workshop *"Try It!"* titled *"Types of Inflation."* This exercise illustrates the case of demand-pull inflation.

Step 3   Read the Graphing Workshop *"Grasp It!"* exercise titled *"Types of Inflation."* This uses a slider bar to demonstrate the difference between cost-push and demand-pull inflation.

Step 4   Play the *"Causation Chains Game"* titled *"Cost-Push and Demand-Pull Inflation."*

Step 5   Listen to the *Ask the Instructor Video Clip"* titled *"Why Was Unemployment Higher in the 1970s than in the 1990s?"* You will learn the causes of cost-push inflation in the 1990s.

Step 6   Listen to the *Ask the Instructor Video Clip"* titled *"Is One Type of Inflation Worse than Another?"* You will learn the difference between demand-pull and cost-push inflation.

Step 7   Read the *EconDebate* article titled *"Should the Strategies of Petroleum Reserve Be Used to Reduce Fluctuations in Oil Prices?"* This article describes 'stagflation' in the 1970s.

The Result   Following these steps, you have learned that demand-pull inflation is caused by increases in the aggregate demand curve and cost-push inflation in the aggregate supply curve.

THE ECONOMIST'S TOOL KIT
Developing the Aggregate Demand and Supply Model

Step one: Draw the aggregate supply curve (AS). In the Keynesian range, the price level is constant during a severe recession. In the intermediate range, the price level rises as full employment approaches. In the classical range, only the price level changes.

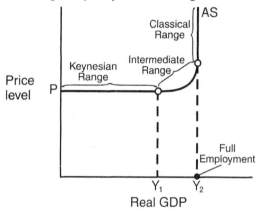

Step two: Include the aggregate demand curve (AD). Where the macroeconomic equilibrium occurs at point E, the equilibrium price level (P^*) measured by a price index and equilibrium real GDP (Y^*) is determined.

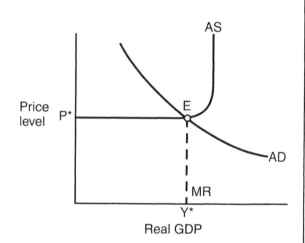

Step three: Demand-pull inflation results from an increase in aggregate demand beyond the Keynesian range. As AD_1 increases to AD_2, the price level rises from P_1^* to P_2^*.

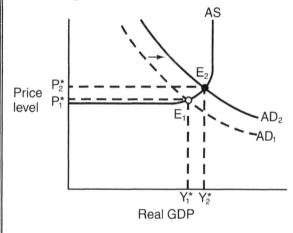

Step four: Cost-push inflation results from a decrease in aggregate supply. As AS_1 decreases to AS_2, the price level rises from P_1^* to P_2^*.

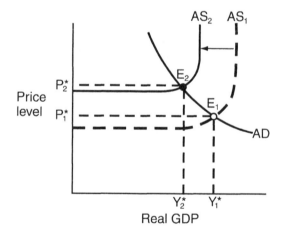

■ COMPLETION QUESTIONS

1. The _____ shows the level of real GDP purchased in the economy at different price levels during a period of time.

2. The _____ is the inverse relationship between the purchasing power of fixed-value financial assets and inflation which causes a shift in the consumption schedule.

3. The _____ assumes a fixed money supply and, therefore, inflation increases the demand for money. As the demand for money increases, the interest rate rises causing consumption and investment spending to fall.

4. The _____ is the inverse relationship between net exports and inflation. An increase in the U.S. price level tends to reduce U.S. exports and increase imports and vice versa.

5. The _____ shows the level of real GDP that an economy produces at different possible price levels. The shape of the aggregate supply curve depends upon the flexibility of prices and wages as real GDP expands and contracts.

6. The _____ of the aggregate supply curve is horizontal because neither the price level or production costs will increase with substantial unemployment in the economy.

7. In the _____ of the aggregate supply curve, both prices and costs rise as real GDP rises toward full employment.

8. The vertical segment of the aggregate supply curve is called the _____.

9. _____ is an economy experiencing inflation and unemployment simultaneously.

■ MULTIPLE CHOICE

1.   Which of the following is *not* a component of the aggregate demand curve?

    a.   Government spending (G).
    b.   Investment (I).
    c.   Consumption (C).
    d.   Net exports (X-M).
    e.   Saving.

2.   The interest-rate effect is the impact on real GDP caused by the direct relationship between the interest rate and the:

    a.   price level.
    b.   exports.
    c.   consumption.
    d.   investment.

3.   Which of the following could *not* be expected to shift the aggregate demand curve?

    a.   Net exports fall.
    b.   Consumption spending decreases.
    c.   An increase in government spending.
    d.   A change in real GDP.

4.   The pre-Keynesian or classical economic theory viewed the long-run aggregate supply curve for the economy to be:

    a.   backward bending at the full-employment level of real GDP.
    b.   positively sloped at the full-employment level of real GDP.
    c.   horizontal at the full-employment level of real GDP.
    d.   none of the above.

5.   Which of the following are beliefs of classical theory?

    a.   Long-run full employment.
    b.   Inflexible wages.
    c.   Inflexible prices.
    d.   All of the above.
    e.   None of the above.

6.   Assuming prices and wages are fully flexible, the aggregate supply curve will be:

   a.   upward sloping, but not vertical.
   b.   vertical.
   c.   horizontal.
   d.   downward sloping.

7.   In the aggregate demand and supply model, the:

   a.   aggregate supply curve is horizontal at full-employment real GDP.
   b.   vertical axis measures real GDP.
   c.   vertical axis measures the average price level.
   d.   All of the above.
   e.   None of the above.

8.   Along the Keynesian range of the aggregate supply curve, a decrease in the aggregate demand curve will decrease:

   a.   only the price level.
   b.   only real GDP.
   c.   both the price level and real GDP.
   d.   real GDP and reduce the price level.

9.   An increase in regulation will shift the aggregate:

   a.   demand curve leftward.
   b.   supply curve rightward.
   c.   supply curve leftward.
   d.   demand curve rightward.

10.   An increase in the price level caused by a rightward shift of the aggregate demand curve is called:

   a.   demand shock inflation.
   b.   supply shock inflation.
   c.   cost–push inflation.
   d.   demand–pull inflation.

Exhibit 1 Aggregate supply and demand curves

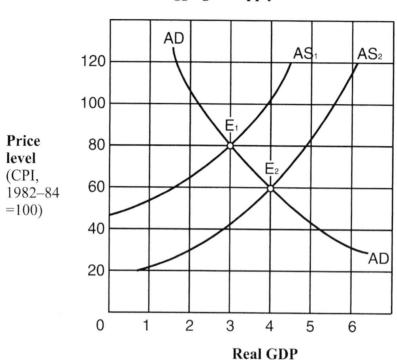

Real GDP
(Billions of dollars per year)

11.   A shift in the aggregate supply curve in Exhibit 1 from AS_1 to AS_2 would be caused by a (an):

a.   decrease in input prices.
b.   increase in input prices.
c.   increase in real GDP.
d.   decrease in real output.

12.   In Exhibit 1, the change in equilibrium from E_2 to E_1 represents:

a.   cost–push inflation.
b.   demand–pull inflation.
c.   price–push inflation.
d.   wage–push inflation.

13.   Keynes theorized that there are _____ when equilibrium real GDP is below the full employment level, which implies a _____ aggregate supply curve.

    a.   highly flexible prices and wages, vertical
    b.   highly flexible prices and wages, horizontal
    c.   fixed prices and wages, vertical
    d.   fixed prices and wages, horizontal

14.   In the intermediate range of the aggregate supply curve, if government expenditures increase caused the aggregate demand curve to shift outward, which of the following is most likely to occur?

    a.   The price level and real GDP will both rise.
    b.   The price level will not change, but real GDP will increase.
    c.   The price level will rise, but real GDP will not change.
    d.   Both the price level and real GDP will not change.

15.   _____ inflation can be explained by an _____ shift in the aggregate _____ curve.

    a.   Demand–pull, inward, demand
    b.   Cost–push, outward, supply
    c.   Demand–pull, outward, supply
    d.   Cost–push, inward, supply

16.   The net exports effect is the inverse relationship between net exports and the _____ of an economy.

    a.   real GDP.
    b.   GDP deflator.
    c.   price level.
    d.   consumption spending.

17.   The popular theory prior to the Great Depression that the economy will automatically adjust to achieve full employment is:

    a.   supply-side economics.
    b.   Keynesian economics.
    c.   classical economics.
    d.   mercantilism.

18.   Other factors held constant, a decrease in resource prices will shift the aggregate:

    a.   demand curve leftward.
    b.   demand curve rightward.
    c.   supply curve leftward.
    d.   supply curve rightward.

19.   Suppose workers become pessimistic about their future employment, which causes them to save more and spend less. If the economy is on the intermediate range of the aggregate supply curve, then:

    a.   both real GDP and the price level will fall.
    b.   real GDP will fall and the price level will rise.
    c.   real GDP will rise and the price level will fall.
    d.   both real GDP and the price level will rise.

20.   The concurrent problems of inflation and unemployment is termed:

    a.   depression.
    b.   downturn.
    c.   deflation.
    d.   demand-pull inflation.
    e.   stagflation.

■ TRUE OR FALSE

1.   T   F   The quantity of real GDP rises with the price level, ceteris paribus.

2.   T   F   The aggregate supply curve shows the relationship between the price level and the level of real GDP produced by the nation's economy.

3.   T   F   The interest-rate effect is the impact on real GDP caused by the inverse relationship between the price level and the interest rate.

4.   T   F   The net exports effect is the direct relationship between net exports and the price level of an economy.

5.   T   F   The Keynesian view is that the aggregate supply curve is vertical.

6.   T   F   The Classical economists believe that prices and wages quickly adjust to keep the economy operating at full employment.

7. T   F   The Classical approach to a downturn in the business cycle was for the government to do nothing.

8. T   F   If aggregate demand equals aggregate supply, macroeconomic equilibrium exists.

9. T   F   An increase in input prices will cause the aggregate supply curve to shift rightward.

10. T   F   A leftward shift in the aggregate supply curve along a fixed aggregate demand curve will cause cost–push inflation.

■ CROSSWORD PUZZLE

Fill in the crossword puzzle from the list of key concepts. Not all of the concepts are used.

ACROSS

3.   High unemployment and rapid inflation.
5.   The aggregate _____ curve represents the level of real GDP purchased by households, businesses, government, and foreigners.
6.   The _____ effect is the impact on total spending (real GDP) caused by the direct relationship between the price level and the interest rate.
7.   The _____ effect is the impact on total spending (real GDP) caused by the inverse relationship between the price level and the real value of financial assets with fixed nominal value.
8.   The _____ effect is the impact on total spending (real GDP) caused by the inverse relationship between the price level and the net exports of an economy.

DOWN

1.   The vertical segment of the aggregate supply curve.
2.   The _____ range is the rising segment of the aggregate supply curve.
3.   The aggregate _____ curve is the level of real GDP supplied by firms.
4.   The _____ range is the horizontal segment of the aggregate supply curve.

■ ANSWERS

Completion Questions

1. aggregate demand curve
2. real balances or wealth effect
3. real interest-rate effect
4. net exports effect
5. aggregate supply curve
6. Keynesian range
7. intermediate range
8. classical range
9. stagflation

Multiple Choice

1. e 2. a 3. d 4. d 5. a 6. b 7. c 8. b 9. c 10. d 11. a 12. a 13. d 14. a 15. d 16. c 17. c 18. d 19. a 20. e

True or False

1. False 2. True 3. False 4. False 5. False 6. True 7. True 8. True 9. False 10. True

Crossword Puzzle

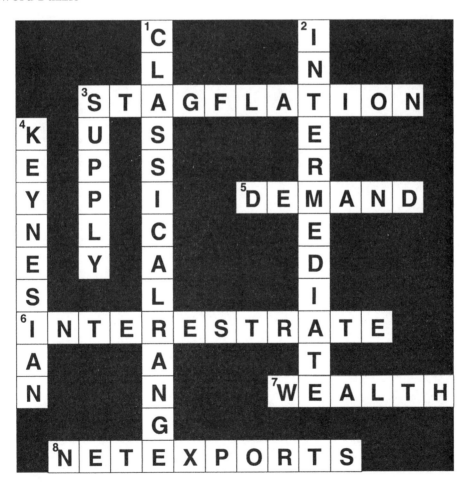

Chapter 10A
The Self-Correcting Aggregate Demand and Supply Model

■ CHAPTER IN A NUTSHELL

The self-correcting aggregate demand and supply model is based on the classical assumption that full-employment is the normal condition for an economy. Aggregate demand (total spending) may change, but in the long run the economy will return to full employment.

The short-run aggregate supply curve is upward sloping because in the short run any change in aggregate demand and therefore the price level do not allow people enough time to adjust to changes in prices. As a result, an increase in aggregate demand when the economy is already at full employment will enable the economy to expand beyond full employment in the short run but at a higher price level. Likewise, a decrease in aggregate demand will decrease the price level and the real GDP level resulting in some unemployment.

However, in the long run (over time) any changes in aggregate demand will have no lasting impact on real GDP (and employment). Suppose there is an increase in aggregate demand. The increase in aggregate demand will increase the price level. In the long run, people will adjust to the higher prices by commanding higher wages and salaries. As they receive them, these higher costs of production shift the short-run aggregate supply curve leftward. We end up back at the full employment real GDP level, but with a higher price level than before. A decrease in aggregate demand will reduce the price level. As wages fall in response to unemployment, costs of production fall and the aggregate supply curve shifts rightward until full employment is re-established. In the long run, any changes in aggregate demand only impact the price level. There is no lasting impact on real GDP.

■ KEY CONCEPTS

> Short-run aggregate supply curve (SRAS)
> Long-run aggregate supply curve (LRAS)

■ MASTER THE LEARNING OBJECTIVES

Please visit the Tucker Xtra! site at http://tuckerxtra.swlearning.com to find the interactive version of the "Master the Learning Objectives" feature.

Describe short-run and long-run adjustments to changes in the aggregate demand curve on the price level, real GDP, and the unemployment rate.

Step 1   Read the sections in your textbook titled *"Why the Short-Run Aggregate Supply Curve is Upward Sloping," "Why the Long-Run Aggregate Supply is Vertical," "Equilibrium in the Self-Correcting AD-AS Model," "The Impact of an Increase in Aggregate Demand,"* and *"The Impact of a Decrease in Aggregate Demand."*

Step 2   Watch the Graphing Workshop *"See It!"* tutorial titled *"Contractionary Gap."* Study why the long-run aggregate supply curve is vertical.

Step 3   Watch the Graphing Workshop *"See It!"* tutorial titled *"Expansionary Gap."* Study the impact of increases and decreases in aggregate demand on short-run and long-run macro equilibrium.

Step 4   Watch the *CNN Video Clip* titled *"Variations on an Enigma"* and analyze how real-world factors related to the SRAS curve.

■ MULTIPLE CHOICE

1.   If nominal wages and salaries are fixed as firms change product prices, the short-run aggregate supply curve is:

   a. vertical.
   b. horizontal.
   c. unit elastic.
   d. negatively sloped.
   e. positively sloped.

2.   An explanation for why the short-run aggregate supply curve is upward-sloping is because:

   a. the quantity of real output supplied is inversely related to aggregate supply.
   b. nominal income are fixed.
   c. the capital-output ratio.
   d. an increase in price will increase the supply of money.

3.   In an economy where nominal incomes adjust equally to changes in the price level, we would expect the long-run aggregate supply curve to be:

   a. vertical.
   b. horizontal.
   c. unit elastic.
   d. negatively sloped.
   e. positively sloped.

4.   In the AD/AS model, a point where the economy's long-run AS curve, short-run AS curve, and AD curve all intersect at a single point represents a point where:

   a. real GDP is equal to its full-employment level.
   b. the conditions of short-run equilibrium are fulfilled.
   c. the conditions of long-run equilibrium are fulfilled.
   d. all of the above.
   e. a and c, but not b.

5.   The intersection between the long-run aggregate supply and aggregate demand curves determines the:

   a. level of full-employment real GDP.
   b. average level of prices (CPI).
   c. money supply.
   d. marginal product.
   e. both a and b.

6.   Beginning from the full-employment level of real GDP, an increase in one of the components of the aggregate demand curve will increase the:

   a. average level of prices (CPI).
   b. unemployment rate.
   c. natural level of real GDP.
   d. level of investment spending.
   e. level of government spending.

7.   Beginning from a position of long-run equilibrium, suppose there is an increase in the aggregate demand curve. Comparing the economy's new long-run equilibrium with its original position, the result would be an increase in:

    a. real GDP.
    b. the price level (CPI).
    c. the unemployment rate.
    d. all of the above.
    e. a and b, but not c.

8.   Suppose that the economy is in a position of short-run equilibrium at a point where real GDP is below the full-employment level. Assuming no further change in aggregate demand and self-correction, the movement to a new long-run equilibrium includes a decrease in which of the following?

    a. The unemployment rate.
    b. The price level (CPI).
    c. The level of nominal wages and salaries.
    d. All of the above.

9.   If an economy is operating at an equilibrium below the level of real GDP, the self-correction model result is that:

    a. unemployment increases.
    b. unemployment falls.
    c. cyclical unemployment increases.
    d. frictional and structural unemployment increase.
    e. a, c and d.

10.   Which of the following causes a leftward shift in the short-run aggregate supply curve?

    a. An increase of goods prices while nominal incomes are unchanged.
    b. An increase in nominal incomes.
    c. An increase of full-employment real GDP.
    d. An increase of personal consumption expenditures while the price level is unchanged.
    e. An increase of personal consumption expenditures while full-employment real GDP is unchanged.

11.   Beginning from a position of long-run equilibrium at the full-employment level of real GDP, the economy's short-run response to an increase in the aggregate demand curve would be:

a. a movement upward along the short-run aggregate supply curve.
b. a movement upward along the long-run aggregate supply curve.
c. a downward shift in the short-run aggregate supply curve.
d. a shift in both the aggregate demand curve and the short-run aggregate supply curve with a movement along the long-run aggregate supply curve.
e. no change, since the economy is already in equilibrium.

Exhibit 1 Macro AD/AS Models

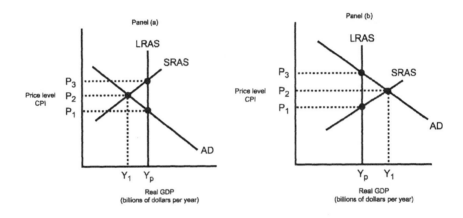

12.   As shown in Panel (a) of Exhibit 1, assume the economy adopts a nonintervention policy. Which of the following would cause the economy to self-correct?

a. Competition among firms for workers increases the nominal wage and SRAS shifts rightward.
b. Long-run equilibrium will be established at Y_1 and P_2.
c. Long-run equilibrium will be established at Y_p and P_3.
d. Competition among unemployed workers decreases nominal wages and SRAS shifts rightward.

13.   In Panel (a) of Exhibit 1, an expansionary stabilization policy designed to move the economy from Y_1 and Y_p would attempt to:

   a. shift aggregate demand to the left by increasing any component of aggregate demand.
   b. shift aggregate demand to the right by increasing any component of aggregate demand.
   c. shift SRAS and LRAS to the right.
   d. do b. and c.

14.   In Panels (a) and (b) in Exhibit 1, the level of real GDP represented by Y_p:

   a. is potential output for this economy.
   b. indicates that the economy is experiencing zero inflation.
   c. indicates that the economy is experiencing a recessionary gap.
   d. would be associated with considerable unemployment.

15.   In Panels (a) and (b) in Exhibit 1, the intersection of AD with SRAS indicates:

   a. a short-run equilibrium.
   b. a long-run equilibrium.
   c. that the economy needs policies to reduce unemployment.
   d. that the economy is at full employment.

Exhibit 2 Macro AD/AS Model

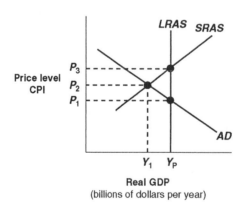

16.   In Exhibit 2, the level of real GDP represented by Y_p:

   a. would be associated with considerable unemployment.
   b. indicates that the economy is experiencing zero inflation.
   c. indicates that the economy is experiencing a recessionary gap.
   d. is potential real GDP for this economy.

17. In Exhibit 2, point P_2, Y_1 represented:

a. that the economy needs policies to reduce unemployment.
b. a long-run equilibrium.
c. a short-run equilibrium.
d. that the economy is at full employment.

18. In Exhibit 2, the self-correction argument is that in the long run competition:

a. from unemployed workers causes an increase in nominal wages and a leftward shift in SRAS.
b. from unemployed workers causes a rightward shift in SRAS.
c. among firms for workers increases nominal wages and this causes a leftward shift in SRAS.
d. among consumers causes an increase in the CPI and a rightward shift in SRAS.

Exhibit 3 Macro AD/AS Model

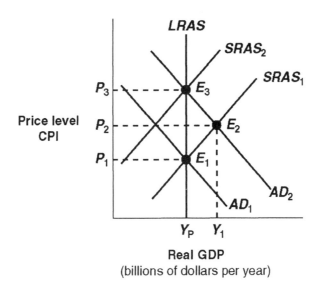

Real GDP
(billions of dollars per year)

19. Given the shift of the aggregate demand curve from AD_1 to AD_2 in Exhibit 3, the real GDP and price level (CPI) in long-run equilibrium will be:

a. P_2, Y_1.
b. P_3, Y_p.
c. P_2, Y_p.
d. P_1, Y_p.

20.   Beginning in Exhibit 3 from long-run equilibrium at point E_1, the aggregate demand curve shifts to AD_2. The economy's path to a new long-run equilibrium is represented by a movement from:

    a. E_1 to E_2 to E_3.
    b. E_3 to E_2 to E_2.
    c. E_1 to E_3 to E_2.
    d. E_2 to E_1 to E_2.

21.   Economic growth is represented in Exhibit 3 by a:

    a.   leftward shift in the long-run aggregate supply curve (LRAS).
    b.   inward shift of the production possibilities curve.
    c.   rightward shift in the long-run aggregate supply curve (LRAS).
    d.   movement along the long-run aggregate supply curve (LRAS).

■ ANSWERS

1. e 2. b 3. a 4. d 5. e 6. a 7. e 8. d 9. b 10. b 11. a 12. d 13. b 14. a 15. a
16. d 17. c 18. b 19. b 20. a 21. c

Chapter 11
Fiscal Policy

■ CHAPTER IN A NUTSHELL

The focus of this chapter is discretionary fiscal policy which involves changes in government purchases or taxes to shift the aggregate demand curve. When the economy suffers from high unemployment because GDP is below the full-employment, the government can follow expansionary fiscal policy and shift the aggregate demand curve rightward by increasing government purchases and/or cutting taxes. When the economy suffers from inflation, the government can follow contractionary fiscal policy and shift the aggregate demand curve leftward by decreasing government purchases and/or raising taxes. The spending multiplier amplifies the amount of the initial change in government purchases, and the tax multiplier amplifies the amount of the initial change in taxes. Automatic stabilizers, such as automatic changes in transfer payments and tax revenues, can reduce variations in unemployment and inflation. The chapter concludes with a discussion of supply-side fiscal policy. According to this theory, government policy should shift the aggregate supply curve to the right. Supply-side economics played an important role in the arguments for the large tax cut in 1981.

■ KEY CONCEPTS

Automatic stabilizers   Fiscal policy
Balanced-budget multiplier   Laffer curve
Budget deficit   Supply-side fiscal policy
Budget surplus   Tax multiplier
Discretionary fiscal policy

■ MASTER THE LEARNING OBJECTIVES

Please visit the Tucker Xtra! site at http://tuckerxtra.swlearning.com to find the interactive version of the "Master the Learning Objectives" feature.

#1 - Explain how fiscal policy combats recession and inflation.

Step 1   Read the section in your textbook titled *"Discretionary Fiscal Policy."*

Step 2   Create a new graph at the Graphing Workshop *"Try It!"* exercise titled *"Changes in Aggregate Demand."* This exercise illustrates how increases in government spending shift the aggregate demand curve and affect real GDP and the price level.

Step 3   Play the *"Causation Chains Game"* titled *"Using Government Spending to Combat a Recession."*

Step 4   Play the *"Causation Chains Game"* titled *"Using Fiscal Policy to Combat Inflation."*

Step 5   Watch the *CNN Video Clip* titled *"About Landings: Controlling the Economy"* and the importance of the timing of fiscal policy.

The Result   Following these steps, you have learned that expansionary fiscal policy increases aggregate demand, while contractionary policy decreases aggregate demand in order to stabilize the economy.

#2 - Understand the impact of automatic stabilizers.

Step 1   Read the section in your textbook titled *"Automatic Stabilizers."*

Step 2   Play the *"Causation Chains Game"* titled *"Automatic Stabilizers."*

Step 3   Read the *EconNews* article titled *"State Spending Impact National Economy."* This article describes automatic stabilizers.

The Result   Following these steps, you have learned federal government expenditures and tax revenues adjust automatically to changes in real GDP and the effect is to offset recessions and inflation.

#3 - Distinguish between Keynesian demand-side and Supply-side effects.

Step 1   Read the section in your textbook titled *"Supply-Side Policy."*

Step 2   Play the *"Causation Chains Game"* titled *"Keynesian Demand-Side Versus Supply-Side Effects."*

Step 3   Read the *EconNews* article titled *"To Spend Or to Save?-That Is the Question."* This article describes supply-slide economics.

The Result   Following these steps, you have learned that the objective of supply-side policy is to increase the aggregate supply curve by, for example, tax cuts and reducing regulations. In contrast, the objective of Keynesian policy is for the federal government to raise spending or cut taxes to influence the aggregate demand curve.

■ COMPLETION QUESTIONS

1.   _____ follows the Keynesian argument that the federal government should manipulate aggregate demand to influence output, employment, and the price level in the economy.

2.   The change in aggregate demand (total spending) resulting from an initial change in taxes is called the _____.

3.   _____ are changes in taxes and government spending which occur in response to changes in the level of real GDP.

4.   A (an) _____ occurs when government revenues exceed government expenditures. A (an) _____ occurs when government expenditures exceed government revenues.

5.   _____ argues that lower taxes encourage work, saving, and investment which shift the aggregate supply curve rightward. As a result, output and employment increase without inflation.

6.   The _____ represents the relationship between the amount of income tax revenue collected by the government and how much revenue will be collected at various tax rates.

7.   The use of government spending and taxed to influence the nation's output, employment, and price level is called _____.

8.   The _____ is an equal change in government spending and taxes, which changes aggregate demand by the amount of the change in government spending.

■ MULTIPLE CHOICE

1.   Fiscal policy is concerned with:

    a.   encouraging businesses to invest.
    b.   regulation of net exports.
    c.   changes in government spending and/or tax revenues.
    d.   expanding and contracting the money supply.

2.   Expansionary fiscal policy occurs when the government:

    a.   increases its spending or increases its tax revenues.
    b.   decreases its spending and increases its tax revenues.
    c.   decreases its spending or reduces its tax revenues.
    d.   none of the above.

Exhibit 1 Aggregate demand and supply model

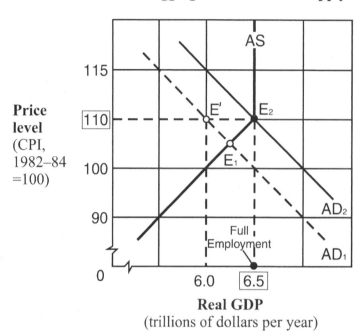

Real GDP
(trillions of dollars per year)

3.   Suppose the economy in Exhibit 1 is in equilibrium at point E_1 and the marginal propensity to consumer (MPC) is 0.75. Following Keynesian economics, the federal government can move the economy to full employment at point E_2 by:

    a.   decreasing government spending by $50 billion.
    b.   decreasing government spending by $200 billion.
    c.   increasing government spending by $125 billion.
    d.   decreasing government spending by $500 billion.
    e.   None of the above.

4.   Suppose the economy in Exhibit 1 is in equilibrium at point E_1 and the marginal propensity to consume (MPC) is 0.75. Following Keynesian economics, the federal government can move the economy to full employment at point E_2 by:

    a.   increasing government tax revenue by approximately $166 billion.
    b.   decreasing government tax revenue by $66 billion.
    c.   increasing government tax revenue by $500 billion.
    d.   decreasing government tax revenue by $500 billion.
    e.   decreasing government tax revenue by approximately $166 billion.

5.   Assume the marginal propensity to consume (MPC) is 0.90 and the government increases taxes by $100 billion. The aggregate demand curve will shift to the:

    a.   left by $1,000 billion.
    b.   right by $1,000 billion.
    c.   right by $900 billion.
    d.   left by $900 billion.
    e.   None of the above.

Exhibit 2 Aggregate demand and supply model

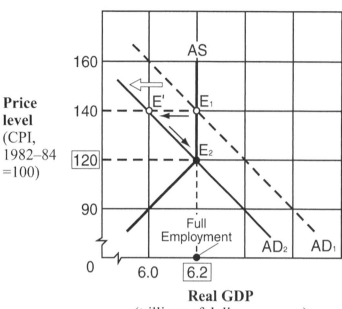

Real GDP
(trillions of dollars per year)

6.   Suppose the economy in Exhibit 2 is in equilibrium at point E_1 and the marginal propensity to consume (MPC) is 0.75. Following Keynesian economics, the federal government can move the economy to point E_2 and reduce inflation by:

a.   increasing government spending by $50 billion.
b.   decreasing government spending by $6 billion.
c.   decreasing government spending by $100 billion.
d.   decreasing government spending by $50 billion.
e.   None of the above.

7.   Suppose the economy in Exhibit 2 is in equilibrium at point E_1 and the marginal propensity to consume (MPC) is 0.75. Following Keynesian economics, the federal government can move the economy to point E_2 and reduce inflation by:

a.   increasing government tax revenue by $6 billion.
b.   decreasing government tax revenue by $6.1 billion.
c.   decreasing government tax revenue by $200 billion.
d.   increasing government tax revenue by approximately $66 billion.
e.   decreasing government tax revenue by approximately $66 billion.

8.   Assume Congress enacts a $500 billion increase in spending and a $500 billion tax increase to finance the additional government spending. The result of this balanced-budget approach is a:

a. $500 billion decrease in aggregate demand.
b. $500 billion increase in aggregate demand.
c. $1,000 billion increase in aggregate demand.
d. $1,000 billion decrease in aggregate demand.

9.   The balanced budget multiplier is always equal to:

a.   1/MPC.
b.   0.75.
c.   0.50.
d.   1.

10.   Automatic stabilizers tend to "lean against the prevailing wind" of the business cycle because:

a.   wages are controlled by the minimum wage law.
b.   federal expenditures and tax revenues change as the level of real GDP changes.
c.   the spending and tax multiplier are constant.
d.   special interests influence government spending and tax revenue legislation.

11.   In the U.S. economy, the effect on federal tax revenues and spending of a decrease in employment is to:

a.   cut tax revenues and raise spending.
b.   cut spending and raise tax revenues.
c.   raise both tax revenues and spending.
d.   cut both spending and tax revenues.

12.   An advocate of supply-side fiscal policy would advocate which of the following?

a.   Subsidies to produce technological advances.
b.   Reduction in regulation.
c.   Reduction in resource prices.
d.   Reduction in taxes.
e.   All of the above.

13.   Which of the following favors government policies to stimulate the economy by creating incentives for individuals and businesses to increase their productive efforts?

    a.   Supply-side economics.
    b.   Keynesian economics.
    c.   Monetarist economics.
    d.   Marxian economics.

14.   Under the Laffer curve theory, changes in the federal tax rate affect:

    a.   tax revenue.
    b.   savings.
    c.   investment.
    d.   incentive to work.
    e.   All of the above.

15.   If the marginal propensity to consume (MPC) is 0.80, and if policy makers wish to increase real GDP by $200 million, then by how much would they have to change taxes?

    a.   -$240 million.
    b.   -$200 million.
    c.   -$180 million.
    d.   -$50 million.
    e.   -$40 million.

16.   Continuing the problem in question 15, if the MPC is still 0.80, and if the goal is to increase real GDP by $200 million, then by how much would government spending have to change to generate this increase in real GDP?

    a. $240 million.
    b. $200 million.
    c. $180 million.
    d. $50 million.
    e. $40 million.

17. Suppose that the economy is operating in a full-employment equilibrium along the vertical section of the aggregate supply curve, but at a higher-than-necessary price level. If the aggregate demand curve must be reduced by $100 billion in order for the price level to decline by the desired 5 percent, and if the marginal propensity to consume is 0.75, then what change in taxes would generate the desired price reduction?

   a. $300 billion.
   b. -$75 billion.
   c. 33.3 billion.
   d. -$25 billion.

18. Supply-side economics calls for:

   a. lower taxes on businesses and individuals.
   b. regulatory reforms to increase productivity.
   c. government subsidies to promote technological advance.
   d. All of the above.

19. During the Reagan administration, the Laffer curve was used to argue that:

   a. the supply-side effects of tax cuts are relatively small.
   b. discretionary tax cuts are unwise because they create stagflation.
   c. lower income tax rates could increase tax revenues.
   d. a "flat tax" would simplify the tax code and stimulate economic growth.

20. A disadvantage of using discretionary fiscal policies to control aggregate demand is that these policies are subject to:

   a. imprecise forecasts.
   b. pressure from interest groups.
   c. time lags.
   d. All of the above are true.

■ TRUE OR FALSE

1. T   F   Fiscal policy is the management of aggregate demand through changes in government purchases and taxes.

2. T   F   The greater the marginal propensity to consume in the economy, the smaller the spending multiplier.

3. T   F   If the marginal propensity to consume is 0.80, the value of the spending multiplier will be 5.

4.   T   F   The tax multiplier is less than the spending multiplier regardless of the value of the marginal propensity to consume.

5.   T   F   Keynesian economics focuses on the role of aggregate spending in determining the level of real GDP.

6.   T   F   Using the aggregate demand and supply model, expansionary fiscal policy will have no effect on the price level but will restore full-employment GDP.

7.   T   F   Using the aggregate demand and supply model, increasing aggregate demand along the classical range of the aggregate supply curve will have no effect on real GDP or the price level.

8.   T   F   Automatic stabilizers are government programs that tend to push the federal budget toward surplus as the real GDP rises and toward deficit as the real GDP falls.

9.   T   F   Supply-siders believe that high tax rates are a disincentive to labor supply.

10.   T   F   The Laffer curve represents on the relationship between real GDP and various possible tax rates.

■ CROSSWORD PUZZLE

Fill in the crossword puzzle from the list of key concepts. Not all of the concepts are used.

ACROSS

4. _____ stabilizers are sometimes referred to as non-discretionary fiscal policy.
5. A _____ emphasizes government policies that increase aggregate supply in order to achieve long-run growth in real output, full employment, and a lower price level.
7. _____ fiscal policy is the deliberate use of change in government spending or taxes to alter aggregate demand and stabilize the economy.
8. _____ policy is the use of government spending and taxes to influence the economy.

DOWN

1. The change in total spending caused by a change in government spending.
2. The change in total spending caused by a change in taxes.
3. The budget _____ is when government expenditures exceed revenues.
6. A budget _____ is when government revenues exceed expenditures.

■ ANSWERS

Completion Questions

1. discretionary fiscal policy
2. tax multiplier
3. automatic stabilizers
4. budget surplus, budget deficit
5. supply-side fiscal policy
6. Laffer curve
7. fiscal policy
8. balanced budget multiplier

Multiple Choice

1. c 2. d 3. c 4. e 5. d 6. d 7. d 8. b 9. d 10. b 11. a 12. e 13. a 14. e 15. d 16. e 17. c 18. d 19. c 20. d

True or False

1. True 2. False 3. True 4. True 5. True 6. False 7. False 8. True 9. True 10. False

Crossword Puzzle

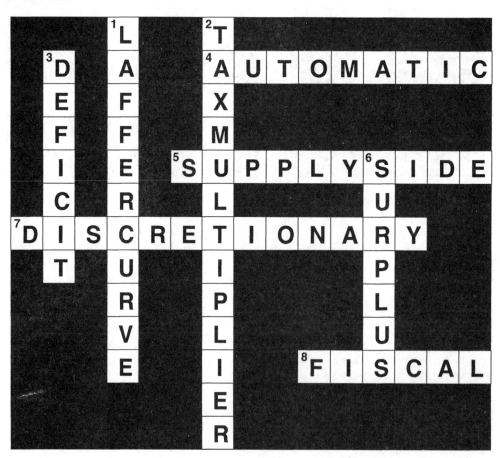

Chapter 12
The Public Sector

■ CHAPTER IN A NUTSHELL

The purpose of this chapter is to examine the economic role of the public sector and how it operates. The chapter begins with data on government spending and tax receipts classified into various categories. Since 1970 total government spending has been about one-third of GDP. The individual and social security taxes are important sources of federal tax revenues, and the sales and property taxes are important sources of state and local governments tax revenues. An interesting point is that citizens in the United States are taxed more lightly than citizens of many of the advanced industrial countries. The chapter also explains two basic tax characteristics-efficiency and equity. The two basic taxation philosophies of fairness are the benefits-received principles and the ability-to-pay principle. The chapter ends with a discussion of public choice theory, which considers how the government performs when it replaces the price system.

■ KEY CONCEPTS

Ability-to-pay principle
Average tax rate
Benefit-cost analysis
Benefits-received principle
Government expenditures
Marginal tax rate

Progressive tax
Proportional or flat-rate tax
Public choice theory
Rational ignorance
Regressive tax

■ MASTER THE LEARNING OBJECTIVES

Please visit the Tucker Xtra! site at http://tuckerxtra.swlearning.com to find the interactive version of the "Master the Learning Objectives" feature.

#1 - Identify major government expenditures and taxes.

Step 1   Read the sections in your textbook titled *"Government Size and Growth,"* *"The Tax Burden,"* and *"The Act of Taxation."*

Step 2   Listen to the *"Ask the Instructor Video Clip"* titled *"Who Really Pays for Social Security?"* You will learn that Social Security is a tax levied on payrolls with a burden double the amount most workers believe they are paying.

Step 3   Listen to the *"Ask the Instructor Video Clip"* titled *"Why Do We Keep the Income Tax If It Is So Unpopular?"* You will learn public choice theory that explains the government's decision-making process.

Step 4   Listen to the *"Ask the Instructor Video Clip"* titled *"How Big Is Government and What Are Its Major Functions?"* You will learn how government expenditures and "tax freedom day" has changed over the years.

Step 5   Read the *EconNews* article titled *"A Taxing Debate."* This article describes a progressive versus a regressive tax.

The Result   Following these steps, you have learned about the relative importance of government expenditures and tax sources. You have also learned that a progressive tax takes a larger percentage of the income of higher income taxpayers, a proportional tax takes about the same percentage of income form all taxpayers, and a regressive tax takes a larger percentage of the incomes of lower income taxpayers.

#2 - Understand public choice theory.

Step 1   Read the section in your textbook titled *"Public Choice Theory."*

Step 2   Listen to the *"Ask the Instructor Video Clip"* titled *"Does It Sometimes Cost Too Much to Save a Life?"* You will learn how benefit-cost analysis applies to real-world situation.

Step 3   Listen to the *"Ask the Instructor Video Clip"* titled *"Does It Sometimes Cost Too Much to Save a Live?"* You will learn how benefit-cost analysis applies to real-world situations.

Step 4   Listen to the *"Ask the Instructor Video Clip"* titled *"Why Do We Keep the Income Tax If It Is So Unpopular?"* You will learn public choice theory that explains the government's decision-making process.

The Result   Following these steps, you have learned that government failure can occur for any of the following reasons: (1) majority voting may not follow benefit-cost analysis, (2) special-interest groups can obtain large benefits and spread their costs over many taxpayers, (3) rational voter ignorance means a sizable portion of the voters will decide not to make informed judgments; (4) bureaucratic behavior may not lead to cost-effective decisions; and (5) politicians suffer from a short time horizon, leading to a bias toward hiding the costs of programs.

■ COMPLETION QUESTIONS

1. The gasoline tax is a classic example of the _____ because users of the highways pay the gasoline tax.

2. Progressive income taxes follow the _____ because there is a direct relationship between the average tax rate and income size. Sales, excise taxes, and flat-rate taxes violate this principle since each results in greater burden on the poor than the rich.

3. The _____ is the tax divided by the income.

4. The _____ is the fraction of additional income paid in taxes.

5. A (an) _____ charges a higher percentage of income as income rises.

6. A (an) _____ charges a lower percentage of income as income rises.

7. A (an) _____ charges the same percentage of income regardless of the size of income.

8. _____ reveals the decision-making process involved in government. For example, government failure can occur because majority voting may not follow _____.

9. _____ are federal, state, and local government outlays for goods and services, including transfer payments.

10. The voter's choice to remain uninformed because the marginal cost of obtaining information is higher than the marginal benefit from knowing it is called _____.

■ MULTIPLE CHOICE

1. Since 1950, total government expenditures in the United States:

    a. grew from about one-quarter to about one-third of GDP.
    b. fell by half, to 10 percent of GDP.
    c. nearly doubled to one-half of GDP.
    d. nearly tripled to about 60 percent of GDP.

2.   Which of the following categories accounted for the largest percentage of total federal government expenditures in 2003?

   a.   Income security.
   b.   National defense.
   c.   Education and health.
   d.   Interest on the national debt.

3.   Which of the following taxes contributed the greatest percentage of total federal government tax revenues in 2003?

   a.   Individual income taxes.
   b.   Corporate income taxes.
   c.   Social Security taxes.
   d.   Excise taxes.

4.   Which of the following countries devote the smallest percentage of its GDP to taxes?

   a.   Germany.
   b.   Sweden.
   c.   The United Kingdom.
   d.   The United States.

5.   "He who pays a tax should receive the benefit from the expenditure financed by the tax." This statement reflects which of the following principles for a tax?

   a.   Inexperience-to-collect.
   b.   Ability-to-pay.
   c.   Benefits-received.
   d.   Fairness of contribution.

6.   Jose pays a tax of $24,000 on his income of $60,000, while Richard pays a tax of $3,000 on his income of $30,000. This tax is:

   a.   a flat tax.
   b.   progressive.
   c.   proportional.
   d.   regressive.

7.   Which of the following can be classified as a regressive tax?

    a.   Excise tax.
    b.   Sales tax.
    c.   Gasoline tax.
    d.   All of the above.

8.   A tax is structured so that the tax as a percentage of income declines as the level of income increases is called a (an):

    a.   flat tax.
    b.   regressive tax.
    c.   progressive tax.
    d.   excise tax.

9.   Which of the following statements is *true*?

    a.   A sales tax on food is a regressive tax.
    b.   The largest source of federal government tax revenue is individual income taxes.
    c.   The largest source of state and local governments tax revenue is sales and excise taxes.
    d.   All of the above are true.
    e.   None of the above are true.

10.   Which of the following offers theories to explain why the government, like the private sector, may also "fail"?

    a.   Social economics.
    b.   Public choice theory.
    c.   Rational expectations theory.
    d.   Keynesian economics.

11.   People who often impose cost on the majority in order to benefit certain groups are called:

    a.   laissez-faire groups.
    b.   encounter groups.
    c.   fair-interest groups.
    d.   special-interest groups.
    e.   none of the above.

12.   The choice of a voter to remain uninformed because the marginal cost of obtaining information is greater than the marginal benefit from obtaining knowledge is called voter:

    a.   irrational ignorance.
    b.   rational ignorance.
    c.   collective interest.
    d.   choice.

13.   Total U.S. government expenditures as a percentage of GDP were largest during which of the following periods of time?

    a.   The Great Depression.
    b.   World War II.
    c.   The Vietnam War.
    d.   The Energy Crisis of the mid- and late-1970s.

14.   Suppose that society had been using a progressive income tax, but shifted to a proportional or true flat tax. If total tax revenues to government were the same under the two plans, who would be made better off and who would be made worse off?

    a.   Those with low incomes would be made better off, and those with high incomes would be made worse off.
    b.   People at all income levels would be better off.
    c.   People at all income levels would be worse off.
    d.   Those with low income would be made worse off, and those with high incomes would be made better off.

15.   Under majority rule, _____ can pass.

    a.   only those public projects that pass a benefit/cost test.
    b.   only those public projects that fail a benefit/cost test.
    c.   some public projects that fail a benefit/cost test.
    d.   no public projects.

16.   The major federal government expenditure is on:

    a.   national defense.
    b.   income security.
    c.   foreign aid.
    d.   the interest expense of the national debt.
    e.   none of the above.

17.   Sharon pays a tax of $4,000 on her income of $40,000, while Brad pays a tax of $1,000 on his income of $20,000. This tax is:

    a.   regressive.
    b.   progressive.
    c.   proportional.
    d.   a flat tax.

18.   Which of the following statements is *true*?

    a.   Sales, excise, and flat-rate taxes violate the ability-to-pay principles of taxation fairness because each results in a greater burden on the poor than the rich.
    b.   Government failure may occur if voters are rationally ignorant.
    c.   Government failure may occur because of special-interest group political pressure.
    d.   All of the above.

■ TRUE OR FALSE

1.   T   F   The term "public sector" refers only to federal government purchases of goods and services.

2.   T   F   The three major revenue sources for the federal government in order of decreasing percentages are individual income taxes, corporate taxes, and Social Security taxes.

3.   T   F   A person who is in a 31 percent marginal tax bracket and has a total taxable income of $100,000 will owe $31,000 in taxes.

4.   T   F   The federal income tax is progressive because the tax rates increase at higher income levels.

5.   T   F   State and local property taxes are regressive.

6.   T   F   The 1986 Tax Reform Act reduced the number of marginal tax rate brackets.

7.   T   F   Cost-benefit analysis can be applied to individual decision-making and to collective or public choice.

8.   T   F   A special interest group cannot impose its will on the majority because the perceived costs and benefits from government programs are the same for both groups.

9.   T   F   A rational person may remain less than fully informed on an issue to be decided in an election.

■ CROSSWORD PUZZLE

Fill in the crossword puzzle from the list of key concepts. Not all of the concepts are used.

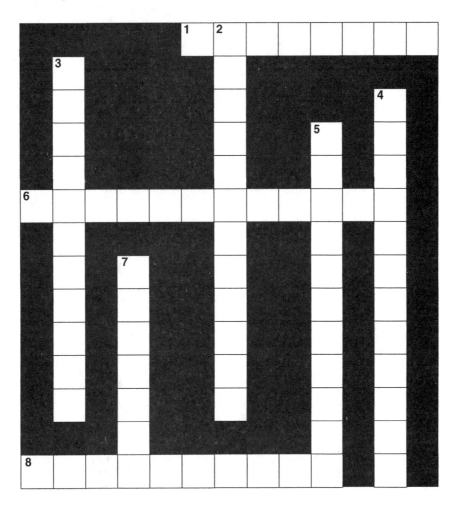

ACROSS

1. _____ ignorance is the voter's choice to remain uninformed because the marginal cost of obtaining information is higher than the marginal benefit from knowing it.

6. The _____ tax that charges rich and poor persons the same percentage of their income.

8. _____ expenditures are federal, state, and local outlays for goods and services.

DOWN

2. The _____ principle is the concept that the rich should pay a greater percentage of income in taxes.

3. A _____ tax charges rich persons a higher percentage of their income.

4. _____ theory is the analysis of government decision-making.

5. _____ analysis is the comparison of the additional rewards and costs of an alternative.

7. The _____ tax rate is the tax divided by income.

■ ANSWERS

Completion Questions

1. benefits-received principle
2. ability-to-pay principle
3. average tax rate
4. marginal tax rate
5. progressive tax
6. regressive tax
7. proportional tax
8. public choice theory, benefit-cost analysis
9. government expenditures
10. rational ignorance

Multiple Choice

1. a 2. a 3. a 4. d 5. c 6. b 7. d 8. b 9. d 10.b 11. d 12. b 13. b 14. d 15. c 16. b 17. b 18. d

True or False

1. False 2. False 3. False 4. True 5. True 6. True 7. True 8. False 9. True

Crossword Puzzle

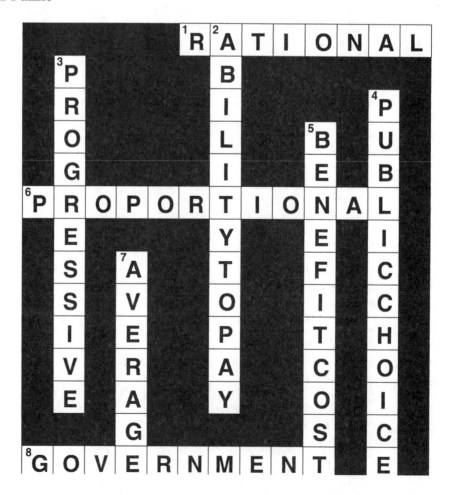

Chapter 13
Federal Deficits, Surpluses, and the National Debt

■ CHAPTER IN A NUTSHELL

The budget deficit is the difference between government expenditures, or outlays, and tax revenues. During the 1960s, the federal government was close to a balanced budget. During the early 1980s, federal budget deficits grew sharply and the public became very concerned about deficits. This situation changed when the federal government had budget surpluses beginning in 1998 and the Congressional Budget Office projected surpluses for years.

The national debt is the result of the federal government's borrowing to finance its deficits. Since 1975, the national debt has skyrocketed from less than $1 trillion to about $6 trillion. Some measures to eliminate, or at least reduce, deficits include spending caps, the balance budget amendment and the debt ceiling. One reason for the concern over the national debt is the percentage of the debt held by foreigners. Paying foreigners interest and principal to finance the debt represents a transfer of wealth from U.S. citizens to citizens of other nations. Another concern is that the federal government's deficit spending might result in a cut in consumption and business investment because the government borrowing may push up the interest rate. In short, the fear is that government budget deficits may "crowd out" private spending.

■ KEY CONCEPTS

Crowding-out effect
Crowding-in effect
Debt ceiling
External national debt
Internal national debt
National debt

■ MASTER THE LEARNING OBJECTIVES

Please visit the Tucker Xtra! site at http://tuckerxtra.swlearning.com to find the interactive version of the "Master the Learning Objectives" feature.

#1 - Know the major steps in federal budgetary process.

Step 1   Read the subsection in your textbook titled *"Federal Budgetary Process."*

Step 2   Play the *"Causation Chains Game"* titled *"Major Steps in the Federal Budgetary Process."*

The Result   Following these steps, you have learned the federal budgetary process.

#2 - Understand financing the national debt and arguments concerning who bears the burden of the national debt.

Step 1   Read the sections in your textbook titled *"Financing the National Debt"* and subsections titled *"Can Uncle Sam Go Bankrupt?* and *"Are We Passing the Debt Burden to Our Children?"*

Step 2   Listen to the *"Ask the Instructor Video Clip"* titled *"How Big Is the National Debt?"* You will learn how the national debt is financed.

Step 3   Listen to the *"Ask the Instructor Video Clip"* titled *"Should We Amend the Constitution to Require a Balanced Budget?"* You will learn different views concerning the issue balancing the federal budget.

Step 4   Watch the *CNN Video Clip* titled *"A Matter of Priorities"* and analyze the debate over what to do with federal budget surpluses.

Step 5   Read the *EconNews* article titled *"Extending the Bush Tax Cuts."* This article describes the debate over acts to control the federal budget.

Step 6   Read the *EconNews* article titled *"Long-Term Affects of the Deficit."* This article describes the impact of the Social Security surplus on the federal deficit.

Step 7   Read the *EconNews* article titled *"Greenspan's Long Term Solution to the Deficit Includes Social Security and Medicare Cuts."* This article describes the argument that entitlement programs like Social Security should be cut to reduce the federal deficit.

The Result   Following these steps, you have learned that the U.S. Treasury issues government securities to finance deficits that increase the national debt. The burden of the debt involves two controversial issues: (1) Can Uncle Sam go bankrupt? and (2) Are we passing the debt burden to our children?

#3 - Explain the meaning of crowding out.

Step 1   Read the subsection titled *"Does Government Borrowing Crowd Out Private-Sector Spending?"*

Step 2   Listen to the *"Ask the Instructor Video Clip"* titled *"What Is Fiscal Policy All About?"* You will learn the problems of using fiscal policy to stabilize an economy, including crowding out.

Step 3   Listen to the *"Ask the Instructor Video Clip"* titled *"What Is 'Crowding-Out' and Is It Important?"* You will learn how spending and borrowing by the government can cancel spending in the private sector.

Step 4   Read the *EconDebate* article titled *"How Should the U. S. Budget Surplus be Used?"* This article describes the crowding-out effect.

The Result   Following these steps, you have learned that crowding out is a reduction in private sector consumer spending and investment because federal government borrowing to finance its deficits increase interest rates.

■ COMPLETION QUESTIONS

1.   The _____ is the dollar amount that the federal government owes holders of government securities. It is the cumulative sum of past deficits.

2.   The percentage of the national debt a nation owes to its own citizens is called
     _____.

3.   _____ is a burden because it is the portion of the national debt a nation owes to foreigners. When interest is paid on this type of debt, this income transfers purchasing power to other nations.

4.   A burden of the national debt caused by the government borrowing to finance its deficit and causing the interest rate to rise is called the _____.
     As the interest rate rises, consumption and business investment fall.

5.   The _____ is the legislated legal limit on the national debt.

■ MULTIPLE CHOICE

1.   The federal budget process begins when federal agencies submit their budget requests to the:

     a.   Congressional Budget Office (CBO).
     b.   Council of Economic Advisors (CEA).
     c.   Department of Commerce (DOC).
     d.   Treasury Department.
     e.   None of the above.

2.   The sum of past federal budget deficits is the:

    a.   GDP debt.
    b.   trade debt plus GDP.
    c.   national debt.
    d.   Congressional debt.

3.   The U.S. Treasury financed federal budget deficits by selling:

    a.   Treasury bonds.
    b.   Treasury notes.
    c.   Treasury bills.
    d.   All of the above.
    e.   None of the above.

4.   Which of the following is *false*?

    a.   The national debt's size decreased steadily after World War II until 1980 and then increased sharply each year.
    b.   The national debt increases in size whenever the federal government has a surplus budget.
    c.   The size of the national debt currently is about the same size as it was during World War II.
    d.   All of the above are false.
    e.   All of the above are true.

5.   Between 1945 and 1980, the national debt as a percent of GDP:

    a.   increased substantially.
    b.   decreased substantially.
    c.   remained about the same.
    d.   increased slightly.
    e.   decreased slightly.

6.   Compared to Germany, France, and the United Kingdom, the national debt as a percentage of GDP in the United States is:

    a.   substantially larger.
    b.   the same.
    c.   slightly larger.
    d.   substantially smaller.

7. The national debt is unlikely to cause national bankruptcy because the:

   a. national debt can be refinanced by issuing new bonds.
   b. interest on the public debt equals GDP.
   c. national debt cannot be shifted to future generations for repayment.
   d. federal government cannot repudiate the outstanding national debt.

8. Since 1945, the net interest payment as a percentage of GDP has increased about:

   a. 50 percent.
   b. 100 percent.
   c. 125 percent.
   d. 200 percent.

9. In recent years, net interest payments as a percentage of GDP has been:

   a. increasing, but by such a small amount that it is not a matter of concern.
   b. falling continuosly.
   c. remained roughly constant.
   d. decreasing slightly.

10. Which of the following U.S. Treasury securities represents internal ownership of the national debt?

    a. Bonds owned by private individuals.
    b. Bonds owned by the Social Security Administration.
    c. Bonds owned by the banks and insurance companies.
    d. All of the above.

11. If all the national debt were owned internally, the federal government would not need to:

    a. worry about raising taxes to pay interest on the national debt.
    b. refinance the national debt.
    c. be concerned about the effect on the distribution of income from interest payments on the national debt.
    d. All of the above are true.
    e. None of the above are true.

12.   Which of the following statements about crowding out is *true*?

a.   It can completely offset the multiplier.
b.   It is caused by a budget deficit.
c.   It is not caused by a budget surplus.
d.   All of the above are true.
e.   None of the above.

13.   With regard to the national debt, to whom does the federal government owe money?

a.   Taxpayers.
b.   Federal government workers.
c.   The Treasurer of the United States.
d.   Investors who buy U.S. Treasury bills, bonds, and notes.

14.   If the national debt rises to the debt ceiling and there is currently a budget _____, then Congress and the President must agree to _____ the debt ceiling or else the federal government will have insufficient funds to pay its bills and will be forced to shut down.

a.   surplus, lower
b.   deficit, raise
c.   deficit, lower
d.   none of the above.

15.   Most of the U.S. national debt is owed to _____. Thus a rising national debt implies that there will be a future redistribution of income and wealth in favor of _____.

a.   foreigners, foreigners.
b.   other U.S. citizens, bondholders
c.   foreigners, those needing government services
d.   other U.S. citizens, those needing government services.

16.   If Congress fails to pass a budget before the fiscal year starts, then federal agencies may continue to operate only if Congress has passed a:

a.   balanced budget amendment.
b.   deficit reduction plan.
c.   tax increase.
d.   continuing resolution.

17.   The national debt is *best* described as the:

    a.   amount by which this year's federal spending exceeds its taxes.
    b.   value of all U. S. Treasury bonds owned by foreigners.
    c.   sum of all federal budget deficits, past and present.
    d.   percentage of GDP needed to finance a country's investment.

18.   Which of the following statements is *true*?

    a.   The national debt as a percentage of GDP is greater today than during any other period in our nation's history.
    b.   A sizeable external national debt will transfer purchasing power away from foreigners to domestic citizens.
    c.   Keynesian theory assumes a total crowding out effect associated with deficit spending.
    d.   U. S. national debt has more than tripled since 1980.

19.   Crowding out occurs when the federal government:

    a.   raises taxes to finance a budget deficit.
    b.   refinances maturing U. S. Treasury bonds.
    c.   borrows by selling bonds to finance a deficit.
    d.   uses a budget surplus to pay off part of the national debt.

20.   The crowding-out effect can be:

    a.   zero.
    b.   partial.
    c.   complete.
    d.   any of the above.

21.   When crowding out occurs, higher government spending results in higher interest rates, which in turn results in:

    a.   higher inflation.
    b.   less consumption and investment.
    c.   a larger debt ceiling.
    d.   more tax revenues.

■ TRUE OR FALSE

1.   T   F   The way to prevent the national debt from growing is for the budget not to be in deficit.

2.   T   F   When we speak of the national debt, we refer to the federal government debt only.

3.   T   F   The entire national debt is owed to U.S. citizens.

4.   T   F   Internal ownership of the debt refers to the portion of the national debt owned by government agencies.

5.   T   F   Less of the federal debt is owned by federal, state, and local governments than is owned by foreigners.

6.   T   F   Bonds owned by financial institutions represent ownership of the national debt by the private sector.

7.   T   F   External debt refers to the portion of the national debt owned by private individuals and internal debt refers to that part owned by the public sector.

8.   T   F   Increased government borrowing stimulates private borrowing because of its effect on interest rates.

9.   T   F   Robert Eisner argues that the absence of adjustment for capital expenditures is one reason the federal deficit is overstated.

■ CROSSWORD PUZZLE

Fill in the crossword puzzle from the list of key concepts. Not all of the concepts are used.

ACROSS

1. The _____ national debt is the portion of the national debt owed to foreigners.
3. The legislated legal limit on the national debt.
4. The _____ effect is a cut in private-sector spending caused by federal deficits.

DOWN

2. The total amount owed by the federal government.
5. The _____ national debt is the portion of the national debt citizens owe to themselves.

■ ANSWERS

Completion Questions

1. national debt
2. internal national debt
3. external national debt
4. crowding-out effect
5. debt ceiling

Multiple Choice

1. e 2. c 3. d 4. d 5. b 6. c 7. a 8. b 9. d 10. d 11. e 12. d 13. d 14. b 15. b 16. d 17. c 18. d 19. c 20. d 21. b

True or False

1. True 2. True 3. False 4. False 5. False 6. True 7. False 8. False 9. True

Crossword Puzzle

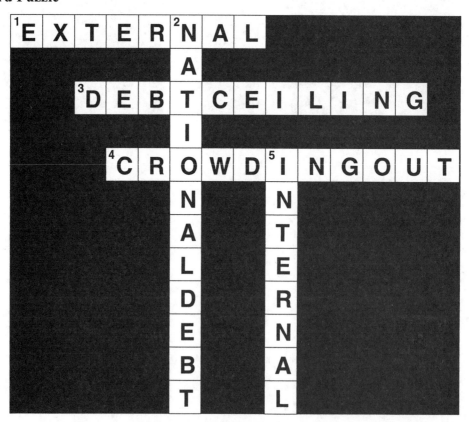

Chapter 14
Money and the Federal Reserve System

■ CHAPTER IN A NUTSHELL

This chapter shifts the attention to money. Money performs these basic functions: it serves as a medium of exchange, a unit of account, and a store or value. Additional requirements are that money be scarce, portable, and divisible. Three measures of the money supply are M1, M2, and M3. M1 is most narrowly defined money supply and it is equal to the sum of currency, travelers checks, and checkable deposits. The chapter then moves to a discussion of the Federal Reserve System. The Fed is the institution responsible for regulating and controlling the money supply. Established in 1913, the Federal Reserve System is composed of a Board of Governors, 12 regional Federal Reserve Banks and commercial banks. The chapter ends with a discussion of the Monetary Control Act of 1980 that gives the Federal Reserve System greater control of nonmember banks and the recent savings and loan crisis.

■ KEY CONCEPTS

Barter	Federal Reserve System
Board of Governors	Fiat money
Checkable deposits	Medium of exchange
Commodity money	M1, M2, M3
Currency	Money
Federal Deposit Insurance Corporation (FDIC)	Monetary Control Act
	Store of value
Federal Open Market Committee (FOMC)	Unit of account

■ MASTER THE LEARNING OBJECTIVES

Please visit the Tucker Xtra! site at http://tuckerxtra.swlearning.com to find the interactive version of the "Master the Learning Objectives" feature.

#1 - Discuss the functions of money and define the money supply.

Step 1   Read the sections in your textbook titled *"What Makes Money **Money**?,"* *"Other Desirable Properties of Money?,"* *"What Stands Behind Our Money,"* and *"The Three Money Supply Definitions."*

Step 2   Listen to the *"Ask the Instructor Video Clip"* titled *"What Has Been Money in the Past and What Is Money Today?"* You will learn about the history of money and the M1 definition of money.

Step 3   Read the *EconNews* article titled *"Making it Tough on Counterfeiters."* This article describes the problem of counterfeiting.

Step 4   Read the *EconNews* article titled *"The Midas Factor."* This article describes the store of value function of money.

The Result   Following these steps, you have learned that money serves as a medium of exchange, unit of account, and store of value. The narrowly defined money supply (M1) consists of currency, traveler's checks and checkable deposits. A broader definition, such as M2, includes savings deposits and small time deposits.

#2 - Discuss the organization and functions of the Federal Reserve System.

Step 1   Read the section in your textbook titled *"The Federal Reserve System," "What a Federal Reserve Bank Does,"* and *"The U.S. Banking Revolution."*

Step 2   Listen to the *"Ask the Instructor Video Clip"* titled *"Why Do People Listen to Alan Greenspan?"* You will learn how the Federal Reserve System is organized and its impact on the economy.

Step 3   Read the *EconNews* article titled *"The Long Term Prospect for Inflation."* This article describes the Federal Open Market Committee.

Step 4   Read the *EconDebate* article titled *"Should U.S. Financial Markets be Deregulated?"* This article describes the Federal Deposit Insurance Corporation (FDIC).

The Result   Following these steps, you have learned that the Federal Reserve System (FED) is the U.S. central bank responsible for controlling the money supply. It also clears checks, regulates banks, circulates currency, protects consumers, and maintains federal government check accounts and gold.

■ COMPLETION QUESTIONS

1.   _____ can be anything that serves as a (1) medium of exchange, (2) unit of account, and (3) store of value.

2.   _____ is the most important function of money. This means that money is widely accepted in payment for goods and services.

3.   _____ is the function of money to measure relative values by serving as a common yardstick for valuing goods and services.

4.   _____ is the property of money to hold its value over time. Money is said to be highly liquid, which means it is readily usable in exchange.

5.   _____ is money that has a marketable value, such as gold and silver. Today, the United States uses fiat money that must be accepted by law, but is not convertible into gold, silver, or any commodity.

6.   _____ is the narrowest definition of money which equals currency plus checkable deposits.

7.   _____ is a broader definition of money which equals M1 plus such as savings deposits and small time deposits.

8.   _____ is an even broader definition of money which equals M2 plus large time deposits of more than $100,000.

9.   The _____ is our central bank and was established in 1913.

10.   The _____ directs the buying and selling of U.S. government securities, which is a key method of controlling the money supply.

11.   _____ is the direct exchange of one good for another good, rather than for money.

12.   Money accepted by law and not because of redeemability or intrinsic value is called _____.

13.   _____ is money, including coins and paper money.

14.   The total of checking account balances in financial institutions convertible to currency "on demand" by writing a check without advance notice is called_____.

15.   _____ is the seven members appointed by the president and confirmed by the U.S. Senate who serve for one nonrenewable 14-year term. Their responsibility is to supervise and control the money supply and the banking system of the United States.

16.   The _____ is the government agency established in 1933 to insure commercial bank deposits up to a specified limit.

17.   A law, formally titled the Depository Institutions Deregulation and Monetary Control Act of 1980, that gives the Federal Reserve System greater control of nonmember banks and makes all financial institutions more competitive is called the _____.

■ MULTIPLE CHOICE

1.   A direct exchange of fish for corn is an example of:

   a.   storing value.
   b.   a modern exchange method.
   c.   barter.
   d.   a non-coincidence of wants.

2.   Which of the following is *not* an example of money used as a unit of account?

   a.   A British pound is worth $3.00.
   b.   Auto repairs for a small business were $3,000 and business travel was $8,000.
   c.   A housewife has a $5,000 credit card limit.
   d.   Gasoline sells for $1.20 per gallon and oil is $5.00 per quart.

3.   Which of the following is a store of value?

   a.   Money market mutual fund share.
   b.   Repurchase agreement.
   c.   All of the above are a store of value.
   d.   None of the above are a store of value.

4.   Anything can be money if it acts as a:

   a.   unit of account.
   b.   store of value.
   c.   medium of exchange.
   d.   All of the above.

5.   Which one of the following statements is *true*?

   a.   Money must be relatively "scarce" if it is to have value.
   b.   Money must be divisible and portable.
   c.   M1 is the narrowest definition of money.
   d.   All of the above.

6.   Which of the following items is included when computing M1?

    a.   Checking accounting entries.
    b.   Currency in circulation.
    c.   Traveler's checks.
    d.   All of the above.
    e.   None of the above

7.   Which of the following is *not* part of M1?

    a.   Checking accounts.
    b.   Coins.
    c.   Credit cards.
    d.   Traveler's checks.
    e.   Paper currency.

8.   Which of the following is considered part of M2?

    a.   Savings deposits.
    b.   Money market mutual fund shares.
    c.   Small time deposits of less than $100,000.
    d.   All of the above.
    e.   None of the above.

9.   Members of the Federal Reserve Board of Governors serve one nonrenewable term of:

    a.   4 years.
    b.   7 years.
    c.   14 years.
    d.   life.

10.   Decisions regarding purchases and sales of government securities by the Fed are made by the:

    a.   FDIC.
    b.   Discount Committee.
    c.   Council of Economic Advisors.
    d.   Federal Funds Committee.
    e.   None of the above.

11.   Which of the following is *not* a protection against bank collapse?

    a.   The gold and silver that backs Federal Reserve notes.
    b.   The Federal Reserve Open Market Committee.
    c.   The Federal Deposit Insurance Corporation.
    d.   The Federal Reserve.

12.   The Monetary Control Act of 1980:

    a.   created less competition among various financial institutions.
    b.   allowed fewer institutions to offer checking account services.
    c.   restricted savings and loan associations to long-term loans.
    d.   all of the above.
    e.   none of the above.

13.   The difference between M1 and M2 is given by which of the following?

    a.   M1 includes currency, coins, gold and silver, whereas M2 does not contain gold and silver.
    b.   M1 is made up of currency, traveler's checks, and money in checkable accounts, whereas M2 contains M1 plus savings deposits and time deposits.
    c.   M1 is limited to currency, whereas M2 contains M1 plus travelers checks and money in checkable accounts.
    d.   M1 includes currency and traveler's checks, whereas M2 contains M1 plus money in checking accounts.

14.   Suppose you transfer $1,000 from your checking account to you savings account. How does this action affect the M1 and M2 money supplies?

    a.   M1 and M2 are both unchanged.
    b.   M1 falls by $1,000 and M2 rises by $1,000.
    c.   M1 is unchanged, and M2 rises by $1,000.
    d.   M1 falls by $1,000 and M2 is unchanged.

15.   The use of a dollar bill to buy a concert ticket represents the use of money as a :

    a.   medium of exchange.
    b.   unit of account.
    c.   store of value.
    d.   all of the above.

16.   Which of the following is *not* a store of value?

    a.   Federal Reserve notes.
    b.   Credit card.
    c.   Debit card.
    d.   Passbook savings deposit.

17.   Which definition of the money supply includes credit cards or plastic money?

    a.   M1
    b.   M2
    c.   M3
    d.   None of the above include credit card balances.

18.   The major protection against sudden mass attempts to withdraw cash from banks is the:

    a.   Federal Reserve.
    b.   Consumer Protection Act.
    c.   deposit insurance provided by the FDIC.
    d.   gold and silver backing the dollar.

19.   The number of presidentially appointed members who sit on the Federal Reserve Board of Governors is:

    a.   none.
    b.   seven.
    c.   nine.
    d.   twelve.

■ TRUE OR FALSE

1.   T   F   Money eliminates the need to barter.

2.   T   F   Any item can successfully serve as money.

3.   T   F   Money is said to be liquid because it is immediately available to spend for goods.

4.   T   F   M2 is actually a smaller amount than M1.

5.   T   F   The Federal Reserve System was created by act of Congress in 1931 in an effort to end a wave of bank failures brought on by the Great Depression.

6.   T   F   A majority of the commercial banks in the United States are members of the Fed.

7.   T   F   Although the chairman of its Board of Governors is appointed by the president, the Fed operates with considerable independence from the executive branch of the government.

8.   T   F   All banks are required to join the Fed.

9.   T   F   Although it has considerable political independence, the Fed is legally a branch of the U.S. Treasury Department.

■ CROSSWORD PUZZLE

Fill in the crossword puzzle from the list of key concepts. Not all of the concepts are used.

ACROSS

3.   The function of money to measure relative value.

6.   Money accepted by law.

7.   Currency, traveler's checks, and checkable deposits.

8.   A government agency established in 1933 to insure commercial bank deposits up to a specified limit.

10.   Anything that serves as a medium of exchange, unit of account, and store of value.

11.   The twelve central banks in the United States.

DOWN

1.   Anything that serves as money and also has market value.

2.   Coins and paper money.

4.   _____ deposits are checking account balances.

5.   The ability to hold money for future purchases.

6.   The committee that buys and sells U.S. securities to control the money supply.

9.   The direct exchange of goods and services.

■ ANSWERS

Completion Questions

1. money
2. medium of exchange
3. unit of account
4. store of value
5. commodity money
6. M1
7. M2
8. M3
9. Federal Reserve System
10. Federal Open Market Committee (FOMC)
11. barter
12. fiat money
13. currency
14. checkable deposits
15. Board of Governors of the Federal Reserve System
16. Federal Deposit Insurance Corporation (FDIC)
17. Monetary Control Act

Multiple Choice Questions

1. c 2. c 3. c 4. d 5. d 6. d 7. c 8. d 9. c 10. e 11. a 12. e 13. b 14. d 15. a 16. b 17. d 18. c 19. b

True or False

1. True 2. False 3. True 4. False 5. False 6. False 7. True 8. False 9. False

Crossword Puzzle

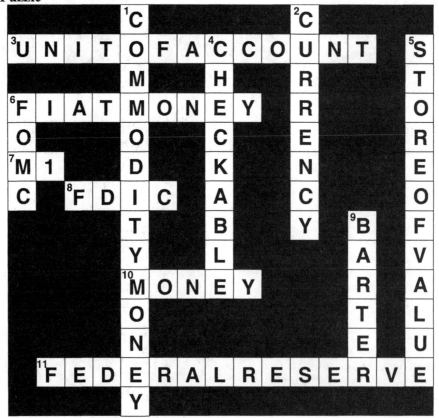

Chapter 15
Money Creation

■ CHAPTER IN A NUTSHELL

This chapter explains how the banking system creates money and thereby influences the money supply. The key to the money creation process is that banks practice fractional-reserve banking. This means banks keep only a fraction of their deposits on reserve as cash and deposits at the Federal Reserve. The minimum required reserves are required by law. A bank creates money by lending or investing its excess of required reserves. The money multiplier gives the maximum change in money (checkable deposits) due to a change in the excess reserves banks hold. The Federal Reserve uses monetary policy to change the money supply. The three basic monetary policy tools are: open market operations, changes in the discount rate, and changes in the required reserve ratio. For example, a sale of government securities by the Fed reduces reserves in the banking system and decreases the money supply. If the Fed wishes to increase the money supply, it might decrease the fraction of deposits that must hold on reserve.

■ KEY CONCEPTS

Discount rate	Money multiplier
Excess reserves	Monetary policy
Federal funds market	Open market operations
Federal funds rate	Required reserves
Fractional reserve banking	Required reserve ratio

■ MASTER THE LEARNING OBJECTIVES

Please visit the Tucker Xtra! site at http://tuckerxtra.swlearning.com to find the interactive version of the "Master the Learning Objectives" feature.

#1 - Explain the role banks play in the creation of the money process.

Step 1   Read the sections in your textbook titled *"Money Creation Begins," "How a Single Bank Creates Money,"* and *"Multiplier Expansion of Money by the Banking System."*

Step 2   Listen to the *"Ask the Instructor Video Clip"* titled *"How Do You Calculate a Bank's Excess Reserves?"* You will learn the amount a bank can lend depends on it excess reserves.

Step 3   Listen to the *"Ask the Instructor Video Clip"* titled *"How Are Banks Different from Other Businesses?"* You will learn that banks are unique because they are regulated corporations that create money by making loans.

The Result   Following these steps, you have learned that banks create new money (checkable deposits) by making loans from their excess reserves. When these loans are deposited in one bank after another throughout the banking system, a money multiplier occurs because the total increase in money supply exceeds the initial increase in excess reserves.

#2 - Understand how the Fed uses its tools to change the money supply.

Step 1   Read the section in your textbook titled *"How Monetary Policy Creates Money."*

Step 2   Play the *"Causation Chains Game"* titled *"Open Market Operations."*

Step 2   Listen to the *"Ask the Instructor Video Clip"* titled *"How Does the Fed Influence Interest Rates?"* You will learn how the Fed controls the money supply using its tools: (1) open market operations, (2) discount rate, and (3) the required reserve ratio.

The Result   Following these steps, you have learned that the Fed's tools of monetary policy are open-market operations, the discount rate, and the required reserve ratio. Using open-market operations, the Fed buys or sells U.S. government securities. The Fed sets the discount rate, which is the rate the Fed charges banks for lending them funds to meet their required reserves. The Fed also sets reserve requirement, which is the percentage of their checkable deposits banks must keep on deposit with the Fed.

#3 - Discuss the shortcomings of monetary policy.

Step 1   Read the section in your textbook titled *"Monetary Policy Shortcomings."*

Step 2   Listen to the *"Ask the Instructor Video Clip"* titled *"Can We Count on Monetary and Fiscal Policy to Smooth Out the Business Cycle?"* You will learn that lags before a policy actually affects the economy are a problem for monetary and fiscal policy.

The Result   Following these steps, you have learned that monetary policy, like fiscal policy, has its limitations.

■ COMPLETION QUESTIONS

1. _____ is the basis of banking today and originated with the goldsmiths in the middle ages.

2. The minimum balance that the Fed requires a bank to hold in vault cash or on deposit with the Fed is called the _____.

3. The percentage of deposits held as required reserves is called the _____.

4. _____ allow a bank to create money by exchanging loans for deposits.

5. The _____ is the maximum change (positive or negative) in checkable deposits (money supply) due to a change in excess reserves.

6. Action taken by the Fed to change the money supply is called _____.

7. _____ are the buying and selling of government securities by the Fed through its trading desk at the New York Federal Reserve.

8. Changes in the _____ occur when the Fed changes the rate of interest it charges on loans of reserves to banks.

9. The _____ is a private market in which banks lend reserves to each other for less than 24 hours.

10. The interest rate banks charge for overnight loans of reserves to other banks is called _____.

■ MULTIPLE CHOICE

1. Which of the following appears on the asset side of a bank's balance sheet?

   a. Excess reserves.
   b. Loans.
   c. Required reserves.
   d. None of the above.
   e. All of the above.

2.   Which of the following is an interest-bearing asset of commercial banks?

    a.   Required reserves.
    b.   Checkable deposits.
    c.   Customer savings accounts.
    d.   All of the above are interest-bearing assets of commercial banks.
    e.   None of the above are interest-bearing assets of commercial banks.

3.   Which of the following is a valid statement?

    a.   Required-reserve ratio = required reserves as a percentage to total deposits.
    b.   Required reserves = the maximum reserves required by the Fed.
    c.   Excess reserves = total reserves plus required reserves.
    d.   All of the above.

4.   Tucker National Bank is subject to a 10 percent required-reserve ratio. If this bank received a new checkable deposit of $2,000, it could make new loans of:

    a. $200.
    b. $1,800.
    c. $2,000.
    d. $20,000.

5.   Tucker National Bank operates with a 20 percent required-reserve ratio. One day a depositor withdraws $500 from his or her a checking account at this bank. As a result, the bank's excess reserves:

    a.   fall by $500.
    b.   fall by $400.
    c.   rise by $100.
    d.   rise by $500.

6.   Assume a simplified banking system subject to a 25 percent required-reserve ratio. If there is an initial increase in excess reserves of $100,000, the money supply:

    a.   increases $100,000.
    b.   increases $400,000.
    c.   increases $125,000.
    d.   decreases $500,000.

7.   If the Fed wishes to increase the money supply then it should:

   a.   increase the required reserve ratio.
   b.   increase the discount rate.
   c.   buy government securities on the open market.
   d.   do any of the above.

8.   Decisions regarding purchases and sales of government securities by the Fed are made by the:

   a.   Federal Funds Committee (FFC).
   b.   Discount Committee (DC).
   c.   Federal Open Market Committee (FOMC).
   d.   Federal Deposit Insurance Commission (FDIC).

9.   The discount rate is the interest rate charged by:

   a.   banks for loans of less than 24 hours.
   b.   banks for overnight loans to other banks.
   c.   the prime rate plus one percent.
   d.   major banks to their best customers.
   e.   none of the above.

10.   The Monetary Control Act of 1980 extended the Fed's authority to:

   a.   impose required-reserve ratios on all depository institutions.
   b.   control the discount rate.
   c.   control the federal funds rate.
   d.   all of the above.

Exhibit 1 Balance sheet of Tucker National Bank

Assets		Liabilities	
Required reserves	$20,000	Checkable deposits	$200,000
Excess reserves	0		
Loans	180,000		
Total	$200,000	Total	$200,000

11.   The required-reserve ratio in Exhibit 1 is:

    a.   10 percent.
    b.   20 percent.
    c.   80 percent.
    d.   100 percent.

12.   Suppose Connie Rich deposits $100,000 into her checking account in the bank shown in Exhibit 1. The result would be a:

    a.   zero change in required reserves.
    b. $10,000 increase in required reserves.
    c. $100,000 increase in required reserves.
    d. $20,000 increase in excess reserves.

13.   Assume the Fed purchases a government security from a private dealer and pays with a Fed check of $100,000. If this check is deposited by the dealer in the bank shown in Exhibit 1, the bank can extend new loans in the amount of:

    a. $20,000.
    b. $90,000.
    c. $100,000.
    d. $120,000.

14.   Assume all banks in the system started with balance sheets as shown in Exhibit 1 and the Fed made a $20,000 open-market purchase. The result would be a (an):

    a. $200,000 expansion of the money supply.
    b. $20,000 expansion of the money supply.
    c. $20,000 contraction of the money supply.
    d.   infinite contraction of the money supply.
    e.   infinite expansion of the money supply.

15.   _____ plus _____ plus _____ equals _____.

    a.   Total deposits, loans, required reserves, excess reserves.
    b.   Loans, required reserves, excess reserves, total deposits.
    c.   Required reserves, total deposits, excess reserves, loans.
    d.   Excess reserves, loans, total deposits, required reserves.

16.   If total deposits at Last Bank and Trust are $100 million, total loans are $70 million, and excess reserves are $20 million, then which of the following is the required reserve ratio?

a.   70 percent.
b.   30 percent.
c.   20 percent.
d.   10 percent.

17.   If Wilma sells a $10,000 Treasury bond to the Fed and deposits the money in he checking account, if the required reserve ratio is 10 percent, and if banks loan out all of their excess reserves, then what is the maximum increase in the money supply after the multiplier effect has fully operated?

a. $1,000.
b. $10,000.
c. $100,000.
d. $1,000,000.

18.   If the required reserve ratio is a uniform 25 percent on all deposits, the money multiplier will be:

a.   4
b.   2.5
c.   0.75
d.   0.25

19.   An increase in required-reserve ratio by the Federal Reserve would:

a.   cause M1 to contract.
b.   cause M1 to expand.
c.   have no effect on M1 or M2.
d.   affect only M2, not M1.

20.   Which of the following policy actions by the Fed would cause the money supply curve to increase?

a.   An open-market sale.
b.   An increase in required-reserve ratios.
c.   A decrease in the discount rate.
d.   All of the above.

■ TRUE OR FALSE

1.   T   F   Banks create money when they make loans.

2.   T   F   The required-reserve ratio is required reserves stated as a percentage of checkable deposits.

3.   T   F   In a system in which all banks have a uniform reserve requirement, the money multiplier is equal to 1 divided by the required-reserve ratio.

4.   T   F   In a simplified banking system, the money multiplier falls as the required-reserve ratio rises.

5.   T   F   As discussed in the text, a bank can extend new loans equal amount by which its excess reserves increase.

6.   T   F   An open-market purchase by the Federal Reserve injects excess reserves into the banking system and allows the money supply to expand.

7.   T   F   An increase in the discount rate by the Federal Reserve causes the money stock to expand.

8.   T   F   Banks that wish to borrow required reserves can turn to the federal funds market.

9.   T   F   The market in which banks make loans of reserves for terms of over one year is called the federal funds market.

10.   T   F   An increase in the required-reserve ratio by the Federal Reserve allows the money stock to contract.

■ CROSSWORD PUZZLE

Fill in the crossword puzzle from the list of key concepts. Not all concepts are used.

ACROSS

1.   The Fed's use of policy tools to change the money supply.
3.   The interest rate the Fed charges on loans of reserves to banks.
6.   Equal to one divided by the required reserve ratio.
7.   _____ operations is the buying and selling government securities by the Fed.

DOWN

2.   Potential loan balances.
4.   The federal funds _____ is the interest rate banks charge for overnight loans of reserves.
5.   The federal funds _____ is the market in which banks lend to each other for 24 hours.

■ ANSWERS

Completion Questions

1. fractional reserve banking
2. required reserve
3. required reserve ratio
4. excess reserves
5. money multiplier
6. monetary policy
7. open market operations
8. discount rate
9. federal funds market
10. federal funds rate

Multiple Choice

1. e 2. e 3. a 4. b 5. b 6. b 7. c 8. c 9. e 10. a 11. a 12. b 13. b 14. a 15. b 16. d 17. c 18. a 19. a
20. c

True or False

1. True 2. True 3. True 4. True 5. True 6. True 7. False 8. True 9. False
10. True

Crossword Puzzle

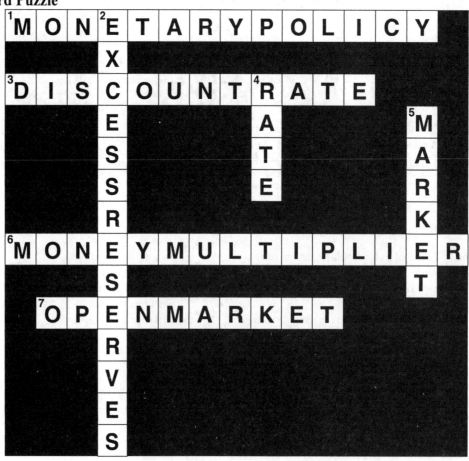

Chapter 16
Monetary Policy

■ CHAPTER IN A NUTSHELL

The previous two chapters provided the foundation for understanding the topic of this chapter: How changes in the money supply affect interest rates and, in turn, real GDP, employment, and the price level. The chapter begins with the Keynesian view that the downward-sloping demand for money curve is determined by these motives: transactions demand, precautionary demand, and speculate demand. The supply of money curve is represented by a vertical line because it is assumed to be established by the Fed regardless of the interest rate. The equilibrium interest rate occurs by the intersection of the money demand and the money supply curves. Assuming the demand for money curve remains fixed, the Fed can use its policy tools to change the interest rate by shifting the vertical money supply curve. In the Keynesian view, changes in the interest rate affects investment, aggregate demand, and, in turn prices, real GDP, and employment. In contrast, the monetarist transmission mechanism argues that changes in the money supply directly cause changes in the aggregate demand curve and thereby changes in prices, real GDP, and employment. Using the quantity theory of money, today's monetarists believe the Federal Reserve should increase the money supply by a constant percentage each year.

■ KEY CONCEPTS

Demand for money curve
Equation of exchange
Monetarism
Precautionary demand for money

Quantity theory of money
Speculative demand for money
Transactions demand for money
Velocity of money (v)

■ MASTER THE LEARNING OBJECTIVES

Please visit the Tucker Xtra! site at http://tuckerxtra.swlearning.com to find the interactive version of the "Master the Learning Objectives" feature.

#1 - Explain how equilibrium is achieved in the money market and the effect on interest rates from changes in the money supply.

Step 1   Read the section in your textbook titled *"The Keynesians View of the Role of Money."*

Step 2   Watch the Graphing Workshop *"See It!"* tutorial titled *"The Money Market."* Study that the money supply (MS) is represented by a vertical line and the equilibrium interest rate is determined by the point where it intersects the demand for money curve (MD).

Step 3   Read the Graphing Workshop *"Grasp It!"* exercise titled *"The Money Market."* This exercise uses a slider bar to demonstrate how changes in the demand for money affect the equilibrium interest rate.

Step 4   Read the Graphing Workshop *"Grasp It!"* exercise titled *"Open Market Operations."* This exercise uses a slider bar to demonstrate how changes in the supply of money affect the equilibrium interest rate.

Step 5   Play the *"Causation Chains Game"* titled *"The Demand for Money Curve."*

Step 6   Play the *"Causation Chains Game"* titled *"The Equilibrium Interest Rate."*

Step 7   Play the *"Causation Chains Game"* titled *"The Effect of Changes in the Money Supply."*

The Result   Following these steps, you have learned that an excess supply of money causes the interest rate to fall and an excess demand for money drives the interest rate upward. Represented by a vertical line, the money supply can be shifted rightward and leftward by the Fed's use of its tools. As a result, the equilibrium rate of interest changes.

#2 - Understand the Keynesian transmission mechanism.

Step 1   Read the subsection titled *"How Monetary Policy Affect Price, Output, and Employment."*

Step 2   Play the *"Causation Chains Game"* titled *"The Keynesian Monetary Policy Transmission Mechanism."*

Step 3   Listen to the *"Ask the Instructor Video Clip"* titled *"Why Should We Care How Fast the Money Supply Grows?"* You will learn the monetary policy transmission mechanism.

Step 4   Read the *EconNews* article titled *"Open, Says the Fed."* This article describes the uses of the discount rate after the September 11 terrorist attacks.

The Result   Following these steps, you have learned that Keynesian policy argues that changes in the money supply affect investment spending, which is a component of the aggregate demand curve. Changes in the aggregate demand curve cause movements along the aggregate supply curve and affect the price level and real GDP.

#3 - Understand the monetarist transmission mechanism.

Step 1   Read the sections in your textbook *titled "The Monetarist View of the Role of Money"* and *"A Comparison of Macroeconomic View."*

Step 2   Play the *"Causation Chains Game"* titled *"The Monetarist Policy Transmission Mechanism."*

Step 3   Watch the *CNN Video Clip* titled *"Braking News"* and analyze the importance of monetary policy affecting the economy through changes in the interest rate.

Step 4   Read the *EconDebate* titled *"Should the Fed Pursue a Fixed Policy Rule?"* This article describes the monetary policy debate between Keynesians and monetarists.

Step 5   Read the *EconDebate* titled *"Does Dollarization Benefit Developing Economics?"* This article describes the effect of the money supply on inflation in developing economies.

The Result   Following these steps, you have learned that Keynesians believe in an indirect relationship in which an increase in the money supply lowers the interest rate which increases investment and then the aggregate demand curve. Monetarists theorize a direct relationship believe changes in the money supply and the aggregate demand curve. Monetarists believe in the equation of exchange (MV=PQ), which argues that changes in the money supply impacts the economy directly through all types of spending. M is the money supply, and V is the velocity of money, or the number of times each dollar is spent in a year. P is the average price level and Q is the quantity of actual output.

THE ECONOMIST'S TOOL KIT
Using Keynesian Monetary Theory

Step one: The money demand curve (MD) intersects the money supply curve (MS) at the equilibrium interest rate (i^*). An excess money demanded causes people to sell bonds, bond prices fall, and the interest rate rises. An excess money supplied causes people to buy bonds, bond prices rise, and the interest rate falls.

Step two: Here the Fed uses its tools to increase the money supply from MS_1 to MS_2 and causes a surplus at i_1^*. As a result, people buy bonds and the interest rate falls to i_2^* at an equilibrium quantity of money Q_2^*.

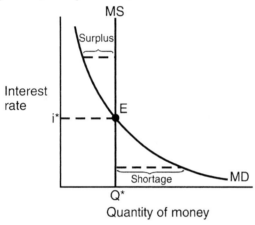

Step three: The Fed's action to lower the equilibrium interest rate from i_1^* to i_2^* causes a movement along the investment demand curve (I) from point A to point B. As a result, businesses increase investment spending from I_1 to I_2.

Step four: Since investment spending is a component the aggregate demand curve, the increase from I_1 to I_2 causes a rightward shift from AD_1 to AD_2. As a result, real GDP rises from Y_1^* to Y_2^* and the price level also rises.

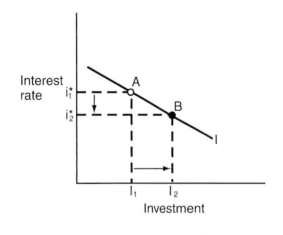

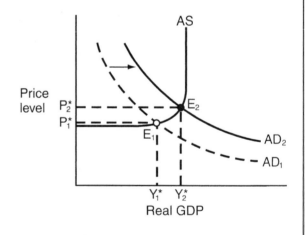

■ COMPLETION QUESTIONS

1. _____ is money held to pay for everyday predictable expenses.

2. _____ is money held to pay unpredictable expenses.

3. _____ is money held to take advantage of price changes in nonmoney assets.

4. The _____ shows the quantity of money people hold at various rates of interest.

5. _____ is the view that changes in monetary policy directly change aggregate demand, and thereby prices, real GDP, and employment.

6. The _____ is an accounting identity which is the foundation of Monetarism. The equation (MV = PQ) states that the money supply times the velocity of money is equal to the price level times real output.

7. The _____ is the number of times each dollar is spent. Keynesians view this concept as volatile and Monetarists disagree.

8. The _____ is a Monetarist argument that the velocity of money, V, and output Q, variables in the equation of exchange are relatively constant. Given this assumption, changes in the money supply yield proportionate changes in the price level.

■ MULTIPLE CHOICE

1. The stock of money people hold to pay everyday predictable expenses is the:

   a. transactions demand for holding money.
   b. precautionary demand for holding money.
   c. speculative demand for holding money.
   d. store of value demand for holding money.

2.   The stock of money people hold to take advantage of expected future changes in the price of bonds, stocks, or other nonmoney financial assets is the:

   a.   unit-of-account motive for holding money.
   b.   precautionary motive for holding money.
   c.   speculative motive for holding money.
   d.   transactions motive for holding money.

3.   In a two-asset economy with money and T-bills, the quantity of money that people will want to hold, other things being equal, can be expected to:

   a.   decrease as real GDP increases.
   b.   increase as the interest rate decreases.
   c.   increase as the interest rate increases.
   d.   none of the above.
   e.   all of the above.

4.   Which of the following statements is *true*?

   a.   The speculative demand for money at possible interest rates gives the demand for money curve its upward slope.
   b.   There is an inverse relationship between the quantity of money demanded and the interest rate.
   c.   According to the quantity theory of money, any change in the money supply will have no effect on the price level.
   d.   All of the above.

5.   In Keynes's view, an excess quantity of money demanded causes people to:

   a.   sell bonds and the interest rate falls.
   b.   increase speculative balances.
   c.   buy bonds and the interest rate rises.
   d.   buy bonds and the interest rate falls.
   e.   none of the above.

6.   Assume the Fed decreases the money supply and the demand for money curve is fixed. In response, people will:

   a.   sell bonds, thus driving up the interest rate.
   b.   buy bonds, thus driving down the interest rate.
   c.   buy bonds, thus driving up the interest rate.
   d.   sell bonds, thus driving down the interest rate.

7.   Using the aggregate supply and demand model, assume the economy is operating along the intermediate portion of the aggregate supply curve. An increase in the money supply will increase the price level and:

a.   raise the interest rate and lower real GDP.
b.   raise both the interest rate and real GDP.
c.   lower both the interest rate and real GDP.
d.   have no effect on the interest rate and real GDP.
e.   none of the above.

Exhibit 1 Money market demand and supply curves

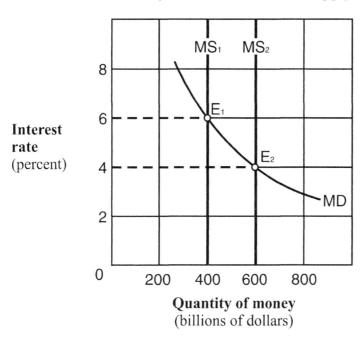

8.   Starting from an equilibrium at E_1 in Exhibit 1, a rightward shift of the money supply curve from MS_1 to MS_2 would cause an excess:

a.   demand for money, leading people to sell bonds.
b.   supply of money, leading people to buy bonds.
c.   supply of money, leading people to sell bonds.
d.   demand for money, leading people to buy bonds.

9.   As shown in Exhibit 1, assume the money supply curve shifts rightward from MS_1 to MS_2 and the economy is operating along the intermediate segment of the aggregate supply curve. The result will be a:

a.   higher interest rate and no effect on real GDP or the price level.
b.   lower investment, lower real GDP, and lower price level.
c.   higher investment, higher real GDP, and higher price level.
d.   higher investment, lower real GDP, and lower price level.

10.   The equation of exchange states:

a. $MV = PQ$.
b. $MP = VQ$.
c. $MP = V/Q$.
d. $V = M/PQ$.

11.   The quantity theory of money of the Classical economists says that a change in the money supply will produce a:

a.   proportional change in the price level.
b.   wide variation in the velocity of money.
c.   less than proportional change in the price level.
d.   greater than proportional change in the price level.

12.   According to Keynesians, an increase in the money supply will:

a.   decrease the interest rate, and increase investment, aggregate demand, prices, real GDP, and employment.
b.   decrease the interest rate, and decrease investment, aggregate demand, prices, real GDP, and employment.
c.   increase the interest rate, and decrease investment, aggregate demand, prices, real GDP, and employment.
d.   only increases prices.

13.   Which of the following is *true*?

a.   Keynesians advocate increasing the money supply during economic recessions but decreaseing the money supply during economic expansions.
b.   Monetarists advocate increasing the money supply by a constant rate year after year.
c.   Keynesians argue that the crowding-out effect is rather insignificant.
d.   Monetarists argue that the crowding-out effect is rather large.
e.   All of the above.

14.   If the Fed reduces the discount rate, which of the following are *most* likely to result?

  a.   The money supply shifts outward, and equilibrium interest rates fall in the money market.
  b.   Investment declines, causing the aggregate demand curve to shift inward to the left, reducing equilibrium real GDP and thus slowing the economy.
  c.   Investment rises, causing the aggregate demand curve to shift outward to the right, increasing equilibrium real GDP and thus accelerating the economy.
  d.   Both a. and b. above are correct.
  e.   Both a. and c. above are correct.

15.   If nominal GDP is $7 trillion, and the money supply is $2 trillion, then what is the velocity of money?

  a.   14.
  b.   7.
  c.   3.5.
  d.   2.

16.   How is modern monetarism different from Keynesianism?

  a.   Monetarists believe that inflation is caused by excessive growth in the money supply, based on the equation of exchange, while Keynesians believe that inflation is caused by excessive growth in aggregate demand.
  b.   Monetarists believe that the velocity of money is predictable, while Keynesians believe it is unstable.
  c.   Monetarists believe that wages and prices are flexible, while Keynesians do not.
  d.   Monetarists believe that crowding-out negates any positive impact of fiscal policy, while Keynesians see a clear impact of fiscal policy on aggregate demand.
  e.   All of the above.

17.   Most monetarists favor:

  a.   frequent changes in the growth rate of the money supply to avoid inflation.
  b.   placing the Federal Reserve under the Treasury.
  c.   a steady, gradual shrinkage of the money supply.
  d.   none of the above.

18.   Assume the demand for money curve is stationary and the Fed increases the money supply. The result is that people:

    a.   increase the supply of bonds, thus driving up the interest rate.
    b.   increase the supply of bonds, thus driving down the interest rate.
    c.   increase the demand for bonds, thus driving up the interest rate.
    d.   increase the demand for bonds, thus driving down the interest rate.

19.   Keynesians reject the influence of monetary policy on the economy. One argument supporting this Keynesian view is that the:

    a.   money demand curve is horizontal at any interest rate.
    b.   aggregate demand curve is nearly flat.
    c.   investment demand curve is nearly vertical.
    d.   money demand curve is vertical.

■ TRUE OR FALSE

1.   T   F   John Maynard Keynes listed three types of motives for people holding money—transactions, precautionary, and speculative.

2.   T   F   The opportunity cost of holding money is properly measured by the rate of interest on financial assets such as bonds.

3.   T   F   An increase in the supply of money, other things being equal, will raise the equilibrium interest rate.

4.   T   F   Starting from equilibrium in the money market, suppose the money supply increases. Other things being equal, this will cause an excess demand for money, leading people to sell bonds.

5.   T   F   If the Fed uses its tools to expand the money supply, bond prices will be bid up and interest rates will fall.

6.   T   F   The transmission mechanism is the effect of changes in monetary policy on prices, real GDP, and employment.

7.   T   F   A rightward shift in the money supply curve is likely to produce a rightward shift in the money demand curve.

8.   T   F   Investment is lowered by expansionary monetary policy.

9.   T   F   If the planned-investment curve is relatively flat, the Keynesian
                conclusion is that the transmission mechanism has little effect on the
                economy.

■ CROSSWORD PUZZLE

Fill in the crossword puzzle from the list of key concepts. Not all of the concepts are used.

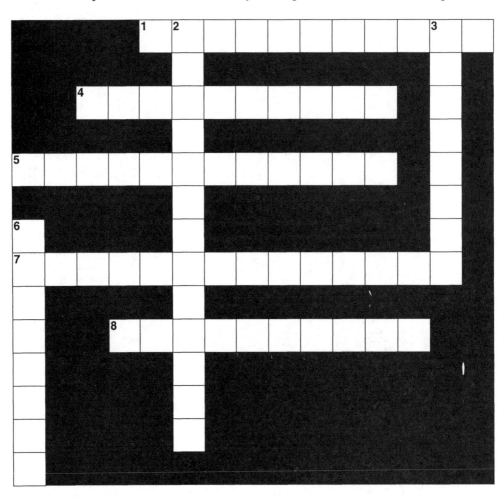

ACROSS

1.   _____ demand is money people hold to take advantage of the future price of nonmoney financial assets.

4.   The demand for _____ is the quantity of money people hold at different possible interest rates.

5.   The _____ demand is money people hold to pay predictable expenses.

7.   The _____ _____ of money states that changes in the money supply yield proportionate changes in the price level.

8.   The theory that changes in the money supply directly affects the economy.

DOWN

2.   The _____ demand is money people hold to pay unpredictable expenses.

3.   The _____ of money is the average number of times a dollar is spent.

6.   The _____ of exchange is MV=PQ.

■ ANSWERS

Completion Questions

1. transactions demand for money
2. precautionary demand for money
3. speculative demand for money
4. demand for money curve
5. Monetarism
6. equation of exchange
7. velocity of money
8. quantity theory of money

Multiple Choice

1. a 2. c 3. b 4. b 5. e 6. a 7. e 8. b 9. c 10. a 11. a 12. a 13. e 14. e 15. c 16. e 17. d 18. d 19. c

True or False

1. True 2. True 3. False 4. False 5. True 6. True 7. False 8. False 9. False

Crossword Puzzle

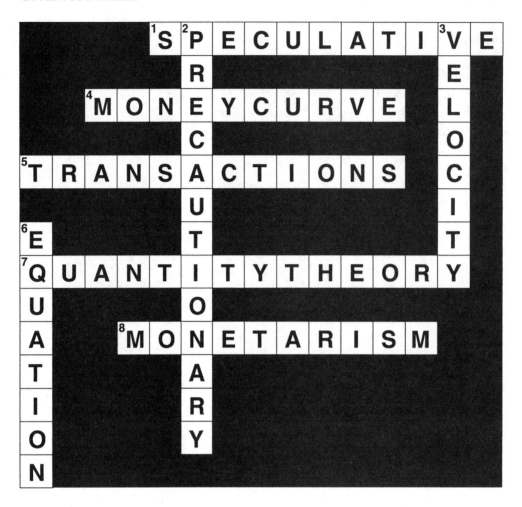

Chapter 16A
Policy Disputes Using the Self-Correcting Aggregate Demand and Supply Model

■ CHAPTER IN A NUTSHELL

Using the self-correcting AD/AS model, this appendix explains the disagreement between the classical and Keynesian schools concerning the use of expansionary and contractionary fiscal policy. The classical school advocates nonintervention fiscal and monetary policy. The classical assumption is that flexible nominal wages will cause the short-run aggregate supply curve (SRAS) to shift and automatically restore the economy to long-run full-employment equilibrium. Instead of a passive role, the Keynesian view is that the federal government and Federal Reserve must take an activist role to restore the economy by shifting the aggregate demand supply curve (AD).

■ MASTER THE LEARNING OBJECTIVES

Please visit the Tucker Xtra! site at http://tuckerxtra.swlearning.com to find the interactive version of the "Master the Learning Objectives" feature.

Understand the difference between classical and Keynesian views of expansionary and contractionary policies.

Step 1   Read the sections in your textbook titled *"The Classical versus Keynesian Views of Expansionary Policy"* and *"Classical versus Keynesian Views of Contractionary Policy."*

Step 2   Watch the Graphing Workshop *"See It!"* tutorial titled *"Expansionary Gap."* Study the difference between a passive and active approach to an inflationary gap.

Step 3   Read the Graphing Workshop *"Grasp It!"* exercise titled *"Expansionary Gap."* This exercise uses a slider bar to demonstrate how changes in aggregate supply or demand can restore an inflationary economy to long-run equilibrium.

Step 4   Create a new graph at the Graphing Workshop *"Try It!"* titled *"Expansionary Gap."* This exercise illustrates the classical argument that the economy will self correct from an inflationary gap to full-employment real GDP in the long run.

Step 5   Watch the Graphing Workshop *"See It!"* tutorial titled *"Closing a Contractionary Gap."* Study the difference between a passive and active approach to a recession.

Step 6   Watch the Graphing Workshop *"See It!"* tutorial titled *"Contractionary Gap."* Study how the federal government can increase aggregate demand using increased spending or tax cuts to combat a recession.

Step 7   Watch the Graphing Workshop *"See It!"* tutorial titled *"Monetary Policy with Aggregate Supply."* Study how the Fed can increase the money supply to increase aggregate demand to combat a recession.

Step 8   Read the Graphing Workshop *"Grasp It!"* exercise titled *"Contractionary Gap."* This exercise uses a slider bar to demonstrate how changes in aggregate supply or demand can restore an economy in recession to long-run equilibrium.

Step 9   Create a new graph at the Graphing Workshop *"Try It!"* titled *"Contractionary Gap."* This exercise illustrates the classical argument that the economy will self correct to full-employment real GDP in the long run.

The Result   Following these steps, you have learned that the classical or noninterventionist school of thought believes that the short-run aggregate supply curve (SRAS) will self correct to long-run full-employment real GDP on the vertical long-run aggregate supply curve (LRAS). The Keynesian or interventionist view is that the fiscal policy and monetary policy must be used to shift the aggregate demand curve to long-run full-employment equilibrium real GDP on LRAS.

■ MULTIPLE CHOICE

1.   Classical theory advocates _____ policy and Keynesian theory advocates _____ policy.

   a. nonintervention; intervention
   b. active; nonstabilization
   c. stabilization; fixed wage
   d. fixed rule; passive

2.   Assuming the economy is experiencing a recessionary gap, classical economists predict that:

   a. wages will remain fixed.
   b. monetary policy will sell government securities.
   c. higher wages will shift the short-run aggregate supply curve leftward.
   d. lower wages will shift the short-run aggregate supply curve rigthward.
   e. none of the above.

3.   Assume the economy is operating at a real GDP above full-employment real GDP. Keynesian economists would prescribe which of the following policies?

   a. Nonintervention
   b. Fixed rule
   c. Contractionary
   d. Expansionary

4.   Assume the economy is experiencing an inflationary gap, Keynesian economists would believe that:

   a. flexible wages will restore full employment.
   b. the federal government should decrease spending to shift the aggregate demand curve leftward.
   c. the Federal Reserve should lower the interest rate.
   d. the federal government should increase spending to shift the aggregate demand curve rightward.

Exhibit 1 Macro AD/AS Model

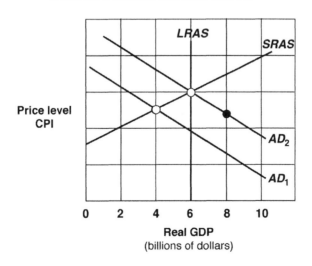

5.   As shown in Exhibit 1, assume the marginal propensity to consume MPC equals 0.75. Using discretionary fiscal policy, federal government spending should be _____ in order to restore the economy to full employment.

   a.   increased by $2 trillion
   b.   decreased by $2 trillion
   c.   increased by $.40 trillion
   d.   increased by $.80 trillion
   e.   increased by $1 trillion

Exhibit 2 Policy Alternative

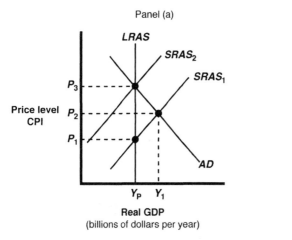
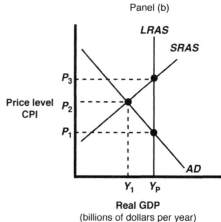

6.   In Panel (a) of Exhibit 2, suppose that the initial equilibrium is at real GDP level Y_1 and price level P_2. At real GDP level Y_1 there is:

   a.   an inflationary gap.
   b.   a recessionary gap.
   c.   full employement.
   d.   long-run equilibrium.

7.   In Panel (a) of Exhibit 2, the economy is initially in short-run equilibrium at real GDP level Y_1 and price level P_2. If the government decides to intervene, it would *most* likely:

   a.   decrease taxes.
   b.   increase transfer payments.
   c.   increase the level of government spending for goods and services.
   d.   decrease the level of government spending for goods and services.

8.   In Panel (a) of Exhibit 2, the economy is initially in short-run equilibrium at real GDP level Y_1 and price level P_2. Classical theory argues that:

   a. $SRAS_1$ will shift to $SRAS_2$ without government intervention.
   b.   lower wages will result in a shift from $SRAS_1$ to $SRAS_2$.
   c.   long-run equilibrium will be established at Y_p and P_3.
   d.   all of the above will take place.

9.   In Panel (b) of Exhibit 2, an expansionary stabilization policy designed to move the economy from Y_1 to Y_p would attempt to shift:

   a.   the aggregate demand curve (AD) leftward.
   b. $SRAS_1$ to $SRAS_2$.
   c.   the aggregate demand curve (AD) rightward.
   d.   the LRAS rightward.

10.   As shown in Panel (b) of Exhibit 2, assume the economy adopts a nonintervention policy. Which of the following would cause the economy to self-correct?

   a.   Competition among firms for workers increases the nominal wage and SRAS shifts rightward.
   b.   Long-run equilibrium will be established at Y_1 and P_2.
   c.   Long-run equilibrium will be established at Y_1 and P_3.
   d.   Competition among unemployed workers decreases nominal wages and SRAS shifts rightward.

■ ANSWERS

1. a 2. d 3. c 4. b 5. e 6. a 7. d 8. d 9. c 10. d

Chapter 17
The Phillips Curve and Expectations Theory

■ CHAPTER IN A NUTSHELL

This chapter explores the Phillips curve, expectations theory, and incomes policies. The Phillips curve indicates the tradeoff between unemployment and inflation. There is a distinction between a short-run and long-run Phillips curve. The short-run Phillips curve slopes downward, and the long run Phillips curve is vertical at full employment.

According to the natural rate hypothesis, the economy will self-correct to the natural rate of unemployment. The long-run Phillips curve is therefore vertical at the natural rate of unemployment. The natural rate hypothesis rests upon the adaptive expectations theory which argue that people believe the best indicator of the future is recent information. As a result, people persistently underestimate inflation when it is accelerating overestimate it while it is slowing down. Therefore, expansionary monetary and fiscal policies designed to reduce the unemployment rate are useless in the long run.

The rational expectations theory argues that people use *all* available information to predict the future, including future monetary and fiscal policies. Systematic and predictable expansionary macroeconomic policies can therefore be negated when businesses and workers anticipate the effects of these policies on the economy. Worse yet, the result is only higher rates of inflation over time. This theory stresses that preannounced, stable policies to achieve a low and constant money supply growth and a balanced federal budget are therefore the best way to lower the inflation rate.

This chapter concludes with a discussion of incomes policies and a comparison of how the monetarists, Keynesians, supply-siders, and new-classicals would cure inflation.

■ KEY CONCEPTS

Adaptive expectations theory
Incomes policies
Jawboning
Natural rate hypothesis
Phillips curve

Political business cycle
Rational expectations theory
Wage and price controls
Wage and price guidelines

■ MASTER THE LEARNING OBJECTIVES

Please visit the Tucker Xtra! site at http://tuckerxtra.swlearning.com to find the interactive version of the "Master the Learning Objectives" feature.

#1 - Understand short-run Phillips curve theory.

Step 1   Read the section in your textbook titled *"The Phillips Curve."*

Step 2   Watch the Graphing Workshop *"See It!"* tutorial titled *"Aggregate Demand, Aggregate Supply, and the Phillips Curve."* Study how changes in the aggregate demand curve are related to the short-run Phillips curve.

Step 3   Read the Graphing Workshop *"Grasp It!"* exercise titled *"Aggregate Demand, Aggregate Supply, and the Phillips Curve."* This exercise uses a slider bar to demonstrate how changes in the aggregate demand curve are related to the short-run Phillips curve.

Step 4   Create a new graph at the Graphing Workshop *"Try It!"* titled *"Aggregate Demand, Aggregate Supply, and the Phillips Curve."* This exercise illustrates how to derive a short-run Phillips curve.

Step 5   Read the *EconDebate* article titled *"Should the Federal Reserve Aim at a Zero Inflation Policy?* This article describes the Phillips curve theory.

The Result   Following these steps, you have learned that the Phillips curve represents an inverse relationship between the unemployment and inflation rates.

#2 - Understand long-run Phillips curve theory and the difference between adaptive and rational expectations.

Step 1   Read the sections in your textbook titled *"The Long-Run Phillips Curve,"* *"The Theory of Rational Expectations, "Applying the AD-AS Model to the Great Expectations Debate,"* *"Incomes Policy,"* and *"How Different Macroeconomic Theory Attack Inflation."*

Step 2   Watch the Graphing Workshop *"See It!"* tutorial titled *"Short-Run and Long-Run Phillips Curves."* Study the difference in short run and long run Phillips curve theory.

Step 3   Read the Graphing Workshop *"Grasp It!* exercise titled *"Short-Run and Long-Run Phillips Curves."* This exercise uses a slider bar to demonstrate how changes in the aggregate demand curve are related to the long-run Phillips curve.

Step 4   Create a new graph at the Graphing Workshop *"Try It!"* titled *"Short-run and Long-Run Phillips Curves."* This exercise illustrates the difference between short-run and long-run Phillips curves.

Step 5   Play the *"Causation Chains Game"* titled *"The Short-Run and Long-Run Phillips Curve."*

Step 6   Listen to the *"Ask the Instructor Video Clip"* titled *"Is the Phillips Curve a Reliable Basis for Stabilization Policy?"* You will learn that the Phillips Curve is not a stable relationship over time.

The Result   Following these steps, you have learned that The natural rate hypothesis argues that the long-run Phillips curve is a vertical line at full-employment real GDP, and adaptive expectations theory is the concept that people persistently improperly estimate changing inflation rates. Rational expectations theory believes that people negate predictable macroeconomic policies.

#3 - Describe the meaning of incomes policies.

Step 1   Read the section in your textbook titled *"Incomes Policy."*

Step 2   Read the *EconNews* article titled *"Let the 'Jawboning' Begin."* This article describes the use of "jawboning" to influence the economy.

The Result   Following these steps, you have learned that incomes policies are federal government policies designed to control nominal wages and prices. These policies include: jawboning, wage and price guidelines and controls.

■ COMPLETION QUESTIONS

1.   The _____ shows an inverse relationship between the inflation rate and the unemployment rate.

2.   The _____ argues the economy will self-correct to the natural rate of unemployment. The long-run Phillips curve is therefore a vertical line at the natural rate of unemployment.

3.   The concept that people believe the best indicator of the future is recent information. As a result, people persistently underestimate inflation when it is accelerating and overestimate it while it is slowing down is called _____.

4.   A _____ is caused by policy makers to improve re-election chances.

5.   The belief that people use all available information to predict the future, including future monetary and fiscal policies. Systematic and predictable macroeconomic policies can therefore be negated when businesses and workers anticipate the effects of these policies on the economy is called _____.

6. _____ are federal government policies designed to affect the real incomes of workers by controlling nominal wages and prices. Such policies include presidential jawboning, wage-price guidelines, and wage-price controls.

7. Voluntary standards set by the government for "permissible" wage and price increases are called _____.

8. _____ is an oratory intended to pressure unions and/ businesses to reduce wage and price increases.

9. _____ are legal restrictions on wage and price increases. Violations can result in fines and imprisonment.

■ MULTIPLE CHOICE

1. The Phillips curve:

   a. is downward sloping.
   b. is upward sloping.
   c. shows there is a tradeoff between unemployment and the inflation rate.
   d. none of the above.

2. Each point on the Phillips curve represent a combination of the:

   a. interest rate and the savings rate.
   b. savings rate and the inflation rate.
   c. consumption rate and the unemployment rate.
   d. inflation rate and the unemployment rate.

3. On a Phillips curve diagram, an increase in the rate of inflation, other things being equal, is represented by a (an):

   a. upward shift of the Phillips curve.
   b. downward movement along Phillips curve.
   c. upward movement along the Phillips curve.
   d. downward shift of the Phillips curve.

4.   Since the 1970s, the Phillips curve has:

    a.   remained stable.
    b.   moved in a clockwise direction.
    c.   been unstable.
    d.   been used as a reliable model to guide public policy.

5.   Under the natural rate hypothesis, expansionary monetary and fiscal policies can at best produce a (an):

    a.   short-run change in the long-run Phillips curve.
    b.   short-run change in the unemployment rate.
    c.   permanent change in the inflation rate.
    d.   permanent change in the unemployment rate.

6.   Under adaptive expectations theory, people expect the rate of inflation this year to be:

    a.   the rate based on predictable and fiscal policies.
    b.   the same as last year.
    c.   zero, regardless of the rate last year.
    d.   All of the above.
    e.   None of the above.

7.   "Preannounced, stable policies to achieve a low and constant money supply growth and a balanced federal budget are therefore the best way to lower the inflation rate." This statement best illustrates the:

    a.   Keynesian theory.
    b.   rational expectations theory.
    c.   adaptive expectations theory.
    d.   supply-side theory.
    e.   incomes policy.

Exhibit 1 Aggregate demand and aggregate supply curves

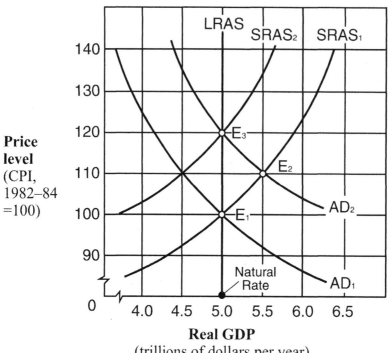

Real GDP
(trillions of dollars per year)

8.   As shown in Exhibit 1, if people behave according to adaptive expectations theory, an increase in the aggregate demand curve from AD_1 to AD_2 will cause the economy to move:

a.   from E_1 to E_2 initially and then eventually move back to E_1.
b.   directly from E_1 to E_2 and then remain at E_2.
c.   directly from E_1 to E_3 and then remain at E_3.
d.   from E_1 to E_2 initially and then eventually move to E_3.

9.   As shown in Exhibit 1, if people behave according to adaptive expectations theory, an increase in the aggregate demand curve from AD_1 to AD_2 will cause the price level to move:

a.   from 100 to 110 initially and then eventually move back to 100.
b.   directly from 100 to 110 and then remain at 110.
c.   directly from 100 to 120 and then remain at 120.
d.   from 100 to 110 initially and then eventually move to 120.

10. As shown in Exhibit 1, if people behave according to adaptive expectations theory, an increase in the aggregate demand curve from AD_1 to AD_2 will cause the price level to move:

   a. directly from 100 to 110 and then remain at 110.
   b. directly from 100 to 120 and then remain at 120.
   c. from 100 to 110 initially and then eventually move back to 100.
   d. from 100 to 110 initially and then eventually move to 120.

11. Incomes policies of the federal government include:

   a. wage-price controls.
   b. wage-price guidelines.
   c. presidential jawboning.
   d. All of the above.
   e. None of the above.

12. Which of the following statements is *true*?

   a. A political business cycle is one created by the incentive for politicians to manipulate the economy to get re-elected.
   b. Adaptive expectations theory argues that the best indicator of the future is recent information.
   c. Incomes policies tend to be ineffective over time.
   d. Incomes policies include jawboning, wage-price guidelines, and wage-price controls.
   e. All of the above.

13. According to adaptive expectations theory and the short-run Phillips curve, which of the following is *true*?

   a. People persistently underestimate inflation when it is both accelerating and slowing down.
   b. People persistently underestimate inflation when it is accelerating, and overestimate inflation when it is slowing down.
   c. People persistently overestimate inflation when it is accelerating and when it is slowing down.
   d. People persistently overestimate inflation when it is accelerating, and underestimate inflation when it is slowing down.

14.   According to rational expectations theory, systematic and predictable expansionary monetary and fiscal policies used to reduce unemployment are _____, and _____.

    a.   useful, can permanently reduce both unemployment and inflation.
    b.   useless, in fact are harmful because the only result is inflation.
    c.   useful, can permanently reduce unemployment at the cost of slightly higher inflation.
    d.   useless, have no impact on either unemployment or inflation.

15.   According to monetarists, the cause of inflation is which of the following?

    a.   Too much money chasing too few goods.
    b.   Aggregate demand that is too high.
    c.   Not enough goods.
    d.   Expectations that policy makers will engage in inflation-inducing policy in the future.

16.   According to Keynesian theory, how do we reduce inflation?

    a.   Allow the economy to self-adjust.
    b.   Increase aggregate supply.
    c.   Change inflationary expectations.
    d.   None of the above.

17.   The long-run Phillips curve:

    a.   is downward sloping.
    b.   is upward sloping.
    c.   shows no tradeoff between unemployment and inflation.
    d.   is horizontal at the natural rate of inflation.

18.   Which of the following statements is *true*?

    a.   The Phillips curve has always been stable.
    b.   If the Phillips curve shifts outward to the right, this illustrates a greater tradeoff between unemployment and inflation.
    c.   Keynesian economics assumes a vertical Phillips curve.
    d.   According to the natural rate hypothesis the Phillips curve is downward sloping.
    e.   All of the above.

19.   According to rational expectations theory, what information do businesses and workers use when they form their expectations regarding inflation?

    a.   Recent events and data.
    b.   Keynesian and monetarist models.
    c.   Forecasts by public-and private-sector economists.
    d.   All the relevant information that is available.

20.   In 1962, President Kennedy persuaded U.S. steel manufacturers to lower their prices. This technique of verbally pressuring unions or businesses without legislation is called:

    a.   Wage and price guidelines.
    b.   wage and price controls.
    c.   an unfair business practice.
    d.   jawboning.

■ TRUE OR FALSE

1.   T   F   The Phillips curve represents an inverse relationship between the inflation rate and the unemployment rate.

2.   T   F   During the 1970s, the inflation rate and the unemployment rate were inversely related.

3.   T   F   The long-run Phillips curve is an upward-sloping line at the natural rate of unemployment.

4.   T   F   According to the adaptive expectations theory, people form their expectations of the future on the basis of future expectations.

5.   T   F   According to the adaptive expectations theory, after many years of rising prices, people tend to ignore past experience in predicting the future rate of inflation.

6.   T   F   Rational expectations theory is the concept that only unanticipated or surprise policies can influence inflation.

7.   T   F   Incomes policies reject wage-price controls and guidelines.

8.   T   F   The "WIN" button approach to breaking a wage-price spiral was proposed by President Ford to a joint session of Congress.

■ CROSSWORD PUZZLE

Fill in the crossword puzzle from the list of key concepts. Not all of the concepts are used.

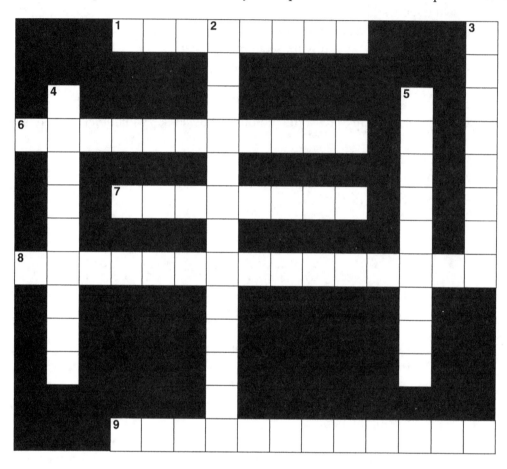

ACROSS

1. _____ expectations theory is the concept that people believe the best indicator of the future is recent information.
6. The _____ hypothesis argues that the economy will self-correct to the natural rate of unemployment.
7. _____ expectations is the belief that people use all available information to predict the future.
8. Presidential jawboning, wage-price guidelines and wage-price controls.
9. Voluntary guidelines set by the government for "permissible" wage and price increases.

DOWN

2. A curve showing an inverse relationship between the inflation rate and the unemployment rate.
3. Wage and price _____ are legal restrictions on wage and price increases.
4. Oratory intended to pressure unions and businesses to reduce wage and price increases.
5. _____ business cycle is caused by policy makers to improve re-election chances.

■ ANSWERS

Completion Questions

1. Phillips curve
2. natural rate hypothesis
3. adaptive expectations theory
4. political business cycle
5. rational expectations theory
6. incomes policies
7. wage and price guidelines
8. jawboning
9. wage and price controls

Multiple Choice

1. c 2. d 3. c 4. c 5. b 6. b. 7. b 8. d 9. d 10. a 11. d 12. e 13. b 14. b 15. a 16. d 17. c 18. b 19. c 20. d

True or False

1. True 2. False 3. False 4. False 5. False 6. True 7. False 8. True

Crossword Puzzle

Chapter 18
International Trade and Finance

■ CHAPTER IN A NUTSHELL

The purpose of this chapter is to explain why international trade is important. The chapter begins by using the production possibilities curve developed in Chapter 2 to demonstrate that international trade permits specialization, and specialization increases total output for countries. Specialization and trade depend on comparative rather than absolute advantage. Trade can be mutually beneficial even if one country has an absolute advantage in the production of all goods. Embargoes, tariffs, and quotas are barriers to free trade. These forms of protectionism are justified on the basis of the infant industries, national security, employment, cheap labor, and other arguments.

The last part of the chapter explains how a country's balance-of-payments records transactions between nations. The balance of trade refers only to part of the balance of payments. A nation is said to have a favorable balance of trade if its exports of merchandise exceed its imports of merchandise. The chapter concludes with an explanation of exchange rates. Assuming a free market for foreign exchange, the exchange rate is determined by the forces of supply and demand.

■ KEY CONCEPTS

Absolute advantage	Embargo
Appreciation of currency	Exchange rate
Balance of payments	Free trade
Balance of trade	Protectionism
Comparative advantage	Quota
Depreciation of currency	Tariff

■ MASTER THE LEARNING OBJECTIVES

Please visit the Tucker Xtra! site at http://tuckerxtra.swlearning.com to find the interactive version of the "Master the Learning Objectives" feature.

#1 - Explain the importance of comparative advantage.

Step 1   Read the sections in your textbook titled *"Why Nations Need Trade,"* and *"Comparative and Absolute Advantage."*

Step 2   Watch the Graphing Workshop *"See It!"* tutorial titled *"Specialization and Trade."* Study the trade in beef and tomatoes between two nations.

Step 3   Read the Graphing Workshop *"Grasp It!"* exercise titled *"Specialization and Trade."* This exercise uses a slider bar to demonstrate how a rancher and a farmer benefit from specialization and trade.

Step 4   Create a new graph at the Graphing Workshop *"Try It!"* titled *"Specialization and Trade."* This exercise illustrates how two countries mutually benefit from trade.

Step 5   Read the *EconNews* titled *"The Wealth of Nations, Part II."* This article describes Adam Smith's theory of division of labor and economic specialization.

Step 6   Read the *EconDebate* article titled *"Does the U. S. Economy Benefit from Foreign Trade?"* The article describes the free trade theory of Adam Smith.

The Result   Following these steps, you have learned that comparative advantage refers to the relative opportunity costs between countries producing the same goods. World output and consumption are maximized when each country specializes in producing and trading goods for which it has a comparative advantage.

#2 - Discuss the argument for and against trade protectionism.

Step 1   Read the sections in your textbook titled *"Free Trade versus Protectionism,"* *"Arguments for Protection,"* and *"Free Trade Agreements."*

Step 2   Listen to the *"Ask the Instructor Video Clip"* titled *"Why Don't We Restrict Trade Among States?"* You will learn the importance of the law of comparative advantage.

Step 3   Listen to the *"Ask the Instructor Video Clip"* titled *"What Are the Arguments for Trade Restrictions?"* You will learn reason for and against the infant industry, national security, and employment arguments for protectionism.

Step 4   Watch the *CNN Video Clip* titled *"The Art of War"* and analyze why countries impose trade restrictions.

Step 5   Read the *EconNews* article titled *"Two Sides to Everything."* This article describes the insourcing of jobs into the United States.

Step 6   Read the *EconNews* article titled *"The Jobs That Went Offshore."* This article describes the loss of jobs overseas.

Step 7   Read the *EconNews* article titled *"U.S. Trade Gap Widens."* This article describes the impact of protectionism.

Step 8   Read the *EconDebate* article titled *"Are Economic Sanctions Effective in Altering a Country's Actions?"* This article describes the debate over trade protectionism.

Step 9   Read the *EconDebate* article titled *"Will the European Monetary Union Succeed?"* This article describes the history of the EMU.

Step 10   Read the *EconDebate* article titled *"Does the U. S. Economy Benefit from the WTO?"* This article describes the history of the World Trade Organization.

The Result   Following these steps, you have learned arguments for embargoes, tariffs, and quotas include the infant industry, national security, employment, and cheap foreign labor arguments. In most cases, economists reject these arguments.

#3 - Understand the meaning of the trade deficit and how exchange rates are determined.

Step 1   Read the sections in your textbook titled *"The Balance of Payments"* and *"Exchange Rates."*

Step 2   Watch the Graphing Workshop *"See It!"* tutorial titled *"Foreign Exchange Market."* Study how the exchange rate for the U.S. dollar in terms of the euro is determined.

Step 3   Read the Graphing Workshop *"Grasp It!"* exercise titled *"Foreign Exchange Market."* This exercise uses a slider bar to demonstrate how the exchange rate for the U.S. dollar in terms of the euro is determined.

Step 4   Create a new graph at the Graphing Workshop *"Try It!"* titled *"Foreign Exchange Market."* This exercise illustrates how a change in the demand for dollars curve affects the market in which U.S. dollars and Mexican pesos are exchanged.

Step 5   Play the *"Causation Chains Game"* titled *"Change in the Supply and Demand Curves for Dollars."*

Step 6   Listen to the *"Ask the Instructor Video Clip"* titled *"How Is Our Economy Related to the Rest of the World?"* You will learn how exchange rates affect the costs of imports and exports.

Step 7   Listen to the *"Ask the Instructor Video Clip"* titled *"How Do We Pay for Imports?"* You will learn the history of the transition form the gold standard to a floating exchange rate system.

Step 8   Listen to the *"Ask the Instructor Video Clip"* titled *"What Causes the Demand for Foreign Exchange to Change?"* You will learn how changes in the supply and demand for currency affect exchange rates.

Step 9   Listen to the *"Ask the Instructor Video Clip"* titled *"Is a 'Strong Dollar' a Good Thing?"* You will learn the impact of a stronger dollar relative to the yen.

Step 10   Watch the *CNN Video Clip* titled *"The Troubles with Trade"* and analyze the causes of large U.S. trade deficits in the 1990s.

Step 11   Watch the *CNN Video Clip* titled *"The Ups and Downs of the Euro"* and analyze a decline in the value of the euro on U.S. firms.

Step 12   Read the *EconNews* article titled *"Trade Deficit Hits Record."* This article describes the growing trade deficit.

The Result   Following these steps, you have learned how the bookkeeping record (balance of payments) and the U. S. balance of trade are computed. Also, you have learned that the price of one currency in units of another currency (the exchange rate) is determined by demand and supply in the foreign exchange market.

THE ECONOMIST'S TOOL KIT
Applying Supply and Demand to Currencies

Step one: Draw a downward-sloping demand curve for dollars. The vertical axis measures the exchange rate. The fewer the yen per dollar, the greater the quantity of dollars demanded by the Japanese.

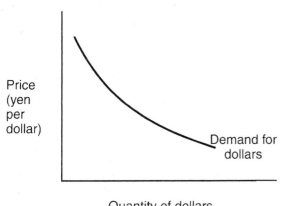

Step two: Draw an upward-sloping supply of dollars. The higher the yen per dollar, the greater the quantity of dollars supplied by U.S. citizens.

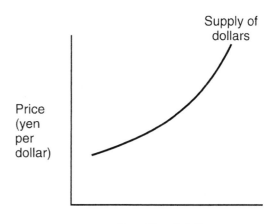

Step three: The exchange rate for dollars is determined by international forces of supply and demand. Suppose some factor, such as a rise in tastes for U.S. exports, increases the demand for dollars from D_1 to D_2. As a result, the value of the dollar rises from P_1^* to P_2^* (dollar appreciates).

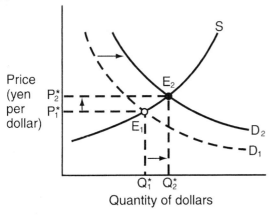

Step four: Here we assume that Japanese imports become more popular in the United States. The result is an increase in the supply of dollars from S_1 to S_2. Thus, the value of the dollar falls from P_1^* to P_2^* (dollars depreciate).

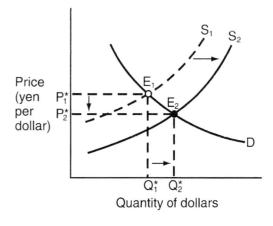

■ COMPLETION QUESTIONS

1. _____ means that each nation specializes in a product for which its opportunity cost is lower in terms of the production of another product and then nations trade.

2. _____ benefits a nation as a whole but individuals may lose jobs and incomes from the competition from foreign goods and services.

3. A government's use of embargoes, tariffs, quotas, and other methods to protect particular domestic industries by imposing barriers that reduce imports is called _____.

4. A (an) _____ prohibits the import or export of particular goods and a (an) _____ discourages imports by making them more expensive. These trade barriers often result primarily from domestic groups that exert political pressure to gain from these barriers.

5. The _____ is a summary bookkeeping record of all the international transactions a country makes during a year. It is divided into different accounts including the current account, the capital account and the statistical discrepancy.

6. The _____ measures only merchandise goods (not services) that a nation exports and imports. It is the most widely reported and largest part of the current account.

7. A (an) _____ is the price of one nation's currency in terms of another nation's currency. The intersection of the supply and demand curves for dollars determines the number of units of a foreign currency per dollar.

8. _____ occurs when a currency becomes worth fewer units of another currency and _____ occurs when a currency becomes worth more units of another currency.

9. A _____ is a limit on the quantity of a good that may be imported in a given time period.

■ MULTIPLE CHOICE

1.   Trade between nations A and B:

    a.   leaves the production possibilities curve of nation A unchanged.
    b.   leaves the production possibilities curve of nation B unchanged.
    c.   increases the consumption possibilities curves of both nations.
    d.   None of the above are true.
    e.   All of the above are true.

2.   A country that has a lower opportunity cost of producing a good:

    a.   has a comparative advantage.
    b.   can produce the good using fewer resources than another country.
    c.   requires fewer labor hours to produce the good.
    d.   all of the above.

3.   Which of the following statements is true?

    a.   Specialization and trade along the lines of comparative advantage allows nations to consume more than if they were to produce just for themselves.
    b.   Free trade theory suggests that when trade takes place any gains made by one nation comes at the expense of another.
    c.   According to the theory of comparative advantage, a nation should specialize in the production of those goods for which it has an absolute advantage.
    d.   All of the above.

4.   A country that can produce a good using fewer resources than another country has a (an):

    a.   lower opportunity cost of producing the good than another country.
    b.   absolute advantage.
    c.   specialization in the production of the good.
    d.   all of the above.

Exhibit 1 Potatoes and wheat output (tons per day)

Country	Potatoes	Wheat
United States	4	2
Ireland	3	1

5.   In Exhibit 1, the United States has an absolute advantage in producing:

a.   wheat.
b.   potatoes.
c.   both.
d.   neither.

6.   In Exhibit 1, Ireland's opportunity cost of producing one unit of wheat is:

a.   1/3 unit of potatoes.
b.   3 units of potatoes.
c.   either a or b.
d.   neither a nor b.

7.   In Exhibit 1, the United States has a comparative advantage in producing:

a.   both.
b.   wheat.
c.   potatoes.
d.   neither.

8.   If each nation in Exhibit 1 specializes in producing the good for which it has a comparative advantage, then:

a.   the United States would produce potatoes.
b.   the United States would produce both potatoes and wheat.
c.   Ireland would produce neither potatoes or wheat.
d.   Ireland would produce potatoes.

9.   Which of the following statements is *true*?

a.   A tariff is a physical limit on the quantity of a good allowed to enter a country.
b.   An embargo is a tax on an imported good.
c.   A quota is a law that bars trade with another country.
d.   When a nation exports more than it imports it is running a balance of trade surplus.

10.   Which of the following is *not* an argument used in favor of protectionism?

a.   To protect an "infant" industry.
b.   To protect domestic jobs.
c.   To preserve national security.
d.   To protect against "unfair" competition because of cheap foreign labor.
e.   To reduce prices paid by domestic consumers.

11.   If U.S. buyers purchased $500 billion of foreign goods and foreign buyers purchased $400 billion of U.S. services, the U.S. balance of trade would be:

   a.   -$100 billion.
   b. $100 billion.
   c. $400 billion.
   d.   none of the above.

12.   Which of the following is included in the current account?

   a.   Net unilateral transfers.
   b.   Merchandise imports.
   c.   Merchandise exports.
   d.   All are included in the current account.
   e.   None are included in the current account.

13.   In the U.S. balance of payments, purchases of foreign assets by U.S. residents are tabulated as a (an):

   a.   unilateral transfer.
   b.   capital outflow.
   c.   current account outflow.
   d.   capital inflow.

14.   If a Japanese stereo priced at 1,000,000 yen can be purchased for $1,000, the exchange rate is:

   a.   1,000 yen per dollar.
   b.   1,000 dollars per yen.
   c.   .01 dollars per yen.
   d.   none of the above.

15.   If the dollar appreciates (becomes stronger) this causes:

   a.   the relative price of U.S. goods to increase for foreigners.
   b.   the relative price of foreign goods to decrease for Americans.
   c.   U.S. exports to fall and U.S. imports to rise.
   d.   a balance of trade deficit for the U.S.
   e.   all of the above.

16.   An increase in inflation in the United States relative to the rate in France would make:

    a.   French goods relatively more expensive in the United States and U.S. goods relatively less expensive in France.
    b.   French goods relatively less expensive in the United States and U.S. goods relatively more expensive in France.
    c.   French goods relatively more expensive in the United States and in France.
    d.   U.S. goods relatively less expensive in the United States and in France.

17.   If there is bilateral currency trade between Japan and the U.S., then as the supply of U.S. dollars on the world foreign exchange market _____, the price of a dollar in terms of Japanese yen will _____.

    a.   increases, fall
    b.   decreases, fall
    c.   increases, increases
    d.   decreases, stays the same.

18.   The value of the U.S. dollar in terms of Japanese yen has declined substantially since the mid-1980's. Which of the following would be consistent with that fact?

    a.   The supply of yen generated by Japanese buying U.S. goods is low, while the demand for yen generated by U.S. consumers buying Japanese goods is high.
    b.   The supply of yen generated by Japanese buying U.S. goods is high, while the demand for yen generated by U.S. consumers buying Japanese goods is low.
    c.   Both the supply of yen and the demand for yen are low because there is relatively little trade between Japan and the U.S.
    d.   None of the above.

19.   If 1 U.S. dollar can be exchanged for 5 euros, then 1 euro can be exchanged for:

    a.   5 cents.
    b.   20 cents.
    c.   50 cents.
    d.   2 dollars.

20.   Which of the following would cause the U.S. dollar to depreciate against the Japanese yen?

    a.   Greater popularity of U.S. exports in Japan.
    b.   A higher price level in Japan.
    c.   Higher real interest rates in the United States.
    d.   Higher incomes in the United States.

■ TRUE OR FALSE

1.   T   F   A country has a comparative advantage in producing a good when it has the lowest opportunity cost of producing that good.

2.   T   F   Absolute advantage governs the potential for gains from trade.

3.   T   F   Trade can increase the consumption possibilities of nations.

4.   T   F   The current account balance tabulates the value of a country's exports of goods and services minus the value of its imports of goods and services.

5.   T   F   A country's imports of merchandise minus its exports of merchandise is reported in the merchandise balance.

6.   T   F   Other things being equal, an increase in U.S. interest rates would be likely to cause an increase in the capital account surplus or a decrease in the capital account deficit.

7.   T   F   Borrowing from foreign banks by U.S. firms represents a capital inflow.

8.   T   F   If the current account and capital account are both in surplus, the official reserve account does *not* have to be in deficit.

9.   T   F   If the yen price of dollars falls, then the dollar price of yen rises.

10.   T   F   An increase in the price level in Japan relative to the price level in the United States will shift the demand curve for dollars leftward and the dollar depreciates or becomes weaker.

■ CROSSWORD PUZZLE

Fill in the crossword puzzle from the list of key concepts. Not all of the concepts are used.

ACROSS

1. _____ of currency is a rise in the price of one currency relative to another.
5. _____ of currency is a fall in the price of one currency relative to another.
7. The balance of _____ is the value of a nation's imports subtracted from exports.
9. The _____ rate is the number of units of one nation's money that equals one unit of another nation's money.
10. A limit on imports.

DOWN

2. The use of restrictions to protect domestic producers.
3. A _____ advantage is the ability of a country to produce a good at a lower opportunity cost.
4. The flow of goods between countries without restrictions or special taxes.
6. The _____ of payments is a bookkeeping record of all international transactions.
8. A law that bars trade with another country.

■ ANSWERS

Completion Questions

1. comparative advantage
2. free trade
3. protectionism
4. embargo, tariff
5. balance of payments

6. balance of trade
7. exchange rate
8. depreciation of currency, appreciation of currency
9. quota

Multiple Choice

1. e 2. a 3. a 4. b 5. c 6. b 7. b 8. d 9. d 10. e 11. d 12. d 13. b 14. a 15. e 16. b 17. a 18. a 19. b 20. d

True or False

1. True 2. False 3. True 4. True 5. False 6. True 7. True 8. False 9. True 10. False

Crossword Puzzle

Chapter 19
Economies in Transition

■ CHAPTER IN A NUTSHELL

The purpose of this final chapter is to explain that pure capitalism and pure communism are polar extremes on a continuum. Most economics are "mixed" and can be classified in reference to one camp or another. The chapter explores the strengths and weaknesses of the three basic types of economic systems including the traditional, command, and market systems. The discussion then turns to the real economic system "isms": capitalism, socialism, and communism. Here, you learn in brief the main ideas of Karl Marx. Also presented in this chapter are of brief discussion of reforms aimed at introducing markets into Cuba, Russia and China. The chapter ends with a discussion of some of the factors that contribute to the Japanese "malaise."

■ KEY CONCEPTS

Capitalism	Invisible hand
Command economy	Market economy
Communism	Mixed economy
Consumer sovereignty	Socialism
Economic system	Traditional economy

■ MASTER THE LEARNING OBJECTIVES

Please visit the Tucker Xtra! site at http://tuckerxtra.swlearning.com to find the interactive version of the "Master the Learning Objectives" feature.

#1 - Describe the strengths and weaknesses associated with different types of economic systems.

Step 1   Read the sections in your textbook titled *"Basic Types of Economic systems,"* and *"The Isms."*

Step 2   Play the *"Causation Chains Game"* titled *"Central Planners Fixing Prices."*

Step 3   Listen to the *"Ask the Instructor Video Clip"* titled *"What Would Happen If Everyone Were Paid the Same?"* You will learn how the production possibilities curve is related to socialism.

Step 4   Read the *EconNews* article titled *"Mickey the Red."* This article describes differences between capitalism and socialism.

Step 5   Read the *EconDebate* titled *"How Should We Reform the Current Tax System?"* This article describes the conflict between equity and efficiency.

#2 - Compare economies in transition.

Step 1   Read the section in your textbook titled *"Comparing Economic Systems."*

Step 2   Watch the *CNN Video Clip* titled "Will the Sun Rise Again?" and analyze the Japanese government's attempts to stimulate its economy.

Step 3   Read the *EconNews* titled *"Japanese Growth Spurred by Chinese Demand."* This article describes the importance of China to Japan's economy.

Step 4   Read the *EconNews* titled *"Chinese Inflation?"* This article describes monetary policy in China.

The Result   Following these steps, you have learned about economies in transition from communism to market economies to allocate goods and services including Cuba, Russia, and China.

■ COMPLETION QUESTIONS

1.   The set of established procedures by which a society answers the What, How, and For Whom to produce goods questions is called a (an) _____.

2.   Three basic types of economic systems include the _____ based on decisions made according to customs, and the _____ which answers the three economic questions through some powerful central authority. In contrast, the uses the impersonal mechanism of the interaction of buyers and sellers through markets to answer the What, How and For Whom questions.

3.   _____ is an economic system in which the factors of production are privately owned, and economic choices are made by consumers and firms in markets.

4.   The determination by consumers of the types and quantities of products that are produced in an economy is called _____.

5.   _____ describes an economy which the government owns the factors of production. The central authorities make the myriad of society's economic decisions according to a national plan.

6.   _____ is an economic system envisioned by Karl Marx to be an ideal society in which the workers own all the factors of production. Marx believed that workers who worked hard would be public spirited and voluntarily redistribute income to those who are less productive.

7.   A phrase that expresses the belief that the best interests of a society are served when individual consumers and producers compete to achieve their own private interests is called a (an) _____.

8.   A _____ is an economic system that answers the What, How, and For Whom questions through a mixture of traditional, command, and market systems.

■ MULTIPLE CHOICE

1.   Which of the following is a basic question by an economic system?

    a.   for whom goods and services are produced.
    b.   how goods and services are produced.
    c.   what goods and services are produced.
    d.   all of the above.
    e.   none of the above.

2.   An economic system that answers the What, How, and For Whom questions using prices determined by the interaction of the forces of supply and demand is a:

    a.   market economy.
    b.   command economy.
    c.   tradtional economy.
    d.   none of the above.

3.   An economic system characterized by private ownership of the factor of production and economic activity coordinated through a system of markets and prices is called:

    a.   capitalism.
    b.   socialism.
    c.   communism.
    d.   none of the above.

4.   Adam Smith's book The Wealth of Nations was published at the time of the:

    a.   Great Depression.
    b.   U.S. Declaration of Independence.
    c.   U.S. Civil War.
    d.   War of 1812.

5.   What famous economist said that the market economy seemed to be controlled by an invisible hand?

    a.   Alfred Marshall.
    b.   Adam Smith.
    c.   Karl Marx.
    d.   Robert L. Heilbroner.

6.   Which of the following is *true* in a market economy?

    a.   Central planners determine answers to the basic economic questions.
    b.   Resources are used efficiently.
    c.   The distribution of wealth is equal.
    d.   Information for production and distribution decisions pass directly to buyers from the government.

7.   Which of the following statements is *true*?

    a.   The doctrine of laissez-faire advocates an economic system with extensive government intervention and little individual decision-making.
    b.   In capitalism income is distributed on the basis of need.
    c.   Adam Smith was the father of socialism.
    d.   Most real-world economies are mixed economic systems.
    e.   The "invisible hand" refers to government economic control.

8.   Which of the following is a characteristic of capitalism?

    a.   Government ownership of all capital.
    b.   Government decision-making is preferred to decentralized decision-making.
    c.   Market determination of prices and quantity.
    d.   Equality of income.

9.   Socialism is correctly described by which of the following statements?

   a.   Central planning is used exclusively to answer the basic economic questions.
   b.   Markets are used exclusively to answer the basic economic questions.
   c.   Tradition answers the basic economic questions.
   d.   Government ownership of many resources and centralized decision-making answers the basic economic questions.

10.   Which of the following is a characteristic of socialism?

   a.   Rejection of central planning.
   b.   Government ownership of all factors of production.
   c.   Government ownership of most of the factors of production.
   d.   Private ownership of all factors of production.

11.   Which of the following statements is *true*?

   a.   The United States today comes closer to the socialist form of economic organization than it does capitalism.
   b.   When central planners set prices above equilibrium for goods and services they create shortages.
   c.   According to Karl Marx, under capitalism, workers would be exploited and would revolt against the owners of capital.
   d.   Adam Smith argued that government's role in society would be to do absolutely nothing.

12.   In Japan, the government agency that combines government and businesses in joint ventures is called.

   a.   MITI.
   b.   GOSPLAN.
   c.   JEEOC.
   d.   KEIRETSU.

13.   Which of the following is *not* an idea advocated by Adam Smith?

   a.   Businessmen conspiring to fix prices is a threat to the price system.
   b.   Pursuit of private self interest with an "invisible hand" is the best way to promote the public interest.
   c.   Government should control the control the economy with an "invisible hand".
   d.   The government should provide for national defense and little else.

14.   In Adam Smith's competitive market economy, the question of what goods to produce is
        determined by:

        a.   the "invisible hand" of the price system.
        b.   businesses.
        c.   unions.
        d.   the government, through laws and regulations.

15.   Karl Marx was a (an):

        a.   19th century German philosopher.
        b.   18th century Russian economist.
        c.   14th century Polish banker.
        d.   19th century Russian journalist.

16.   Who was one of the first proponents of employing market economies instead of
        command economies?

        a.   Robert Heilbroner
        b.   Karl Marx
        c.   Jeffrey Sachs
        d.   Adam Smith

17.   What type of economic system is commonly described as being controlled by an
        "invisible hand'?

        a.   A traditional economy.
        b.   A command economy.
        c.   A market economy.
        d.   A communist economy.

18.   Who predicted that the exploitation of workers would cause capitalism to self-destruct?

        a.   Milton Friedman.
        b.   Robert Heilbroner.
        c.   Karl Marx.
        d.   Adam Smith.

19.   Which of the following is one common criticism of capitalism?

    a.   Poor product quality and little product diversity.
    b.   Inefficiency of nationalized industries.
    c.   Inability to adjust quickly to changing economic conditions.
    d.   Inadequate environmental protection.

20.   Socialism is an economic system characterized by:

    a.   private ownership of resources and market decision-making.
    b.   government ownership of resources and centralized decision-making.
    c.   cooperation, sharing, and little central government.
    d.   a complex structure of rules and traditions that dictates decision-making.

■ TRUE OR FALSE

1.   T   F   A traditional system solves basic economic questions by long-standing customs.

2.   T   F   A traditional system operates based on the self-interest of buyers and sellers.

3.   T   F   A command system uses a group of planners or central authority to make basic economic decisions.

4.   T   F   The command system relies on prices set by firms on the basis of consumer demands.

5.   T   F   When the official price for goods and services is below the equilibrium price in a market, prices no longer perform their rationing function efficiently.

6.   T   F   Adam Smith believed that a nation would produce the maximum wealth by relying on government to make public interest economic decisions.

7.   T   F   A market system does not operate based on self-interest.

8.   T   F   In the real world, countries use a mixture of the three basic types of economic systems.

9.   T   F   Under socialism, no markets can operate at all.

10.   T   F   Karl Marx viewed socialism only as a transition to the ideal state of communism.

11.   T   F   In Marx's ideal state of communism there would be no haves and have-nots.

■ CROSSWORD PUZZLE

Fill in the crossword puzzle from the list of key concepts. Not all concepts are used.

ACROSS

4. An economic system characterized by private ownership.
6. A _____ economy is a system where a central authority answers the basic economic questions.
7. A phrase that expresses the belief that the best interests of a society are served when individual consumers and producers compete to achieve their own private interests.
8. A _____ economy is a mix of traditional, command, and market systems.
9. A _____ economy is a system that answers the basic economic questions the way they have always been answered.

DOWN

1. A stateless, classless economic system envisioned by Karl Marx as the ideal society.
2. An economic system characterized by government ownership of resources and centralized decision-making.
3. The way society organizes to answer the basic economic questions.
5. Consumer _____ is the freedom of consumers to cast their dollar votes in markets.

■ ANSWERS

Completion Questions

1. economic system
2. traditional economy, command economy, market economy
3. capitalism
4. consumer sovereignty
5. socialism
6. communism
7. invisible hand
8. mixed economy

Multiple Choice

1. d 2. a 3. a 4. b 5. b 6. b 7. d 8. c 9. d 10. c 11. c 12. a 13. c 14. a 15. a 16. d 17. c 18. c 19. d 20. b

True or False

1. True 2. False 3. True 4. False 5. True 6. False 7. False 8. True 9. False 10. True 11. True

Crossword Puzzle

Chapter 20
Growth and the Less Developed Countries

■ CHAPTER IN A NUTSHELL

Economic growth and economic development are related, but somewhat different, concepts. Growth is measured quantitatively by GDP per capita. Development includes GDP per capita but also incorporates quality-of-life measures such as life expectancy, literacy rates, and per capita energy consumption.

Growth and development are a result of a complex process that is determined by five major factors: (1) natural resources, (2) human resources, (3) capital, (4) technological progress, and (5) the political environment. Although there is no single correct strategy for economic growth and development, the experience of the "Four Tigers of the Pacific Rim" (sometimes called the "Asian Tigers") might suggest what might be necessary.

GDP per capita provides a general index of a country's standard of living. GDP per capita comparisons are subject to four problems: (1) The accuracy of LDC data is questionable, (2) GDP ignores the degree of income distribution, (3) Changes in exchange rates affect gaps between countries, and (4) there is no adjustment for the differences in cost of living between countries.

Unlike industrially advanced nations (IACs), less developed countries (LDCs) have a low GDP per capita and output is produced without large amounts of technologically advanced capital and well-educated labor. The LDCs account for three-fourths of the world's population.

The "vicious circle of poverty" is a trap in which the LDC is too poor to save money and therefore it cannot invest enough to significantly increase its production possibilities. As a result the LDC remains poor. Consequently, many LDCs are looking for external sources of funds in the form of foreign private investment, foreign aid, and foreign loans.

■ KEY CONCEPTS

Agency for International Development
Foreign aid
GDP per capita
Industrially advanced countries (IACs)
Infrastructure

International Monetary Fund
Less developed countries (LDCs)
New International Economic Order
Vicious circle of poverty
World Bank

■ MASTER THE LEARNING OBJECTIVES

Please visit the Tucker Xtra! site at http://tuckerxtra.swlearning.com to find the interactive version of the "Master the Learning Objectives" feature.

#1 - Compare characteristics of industrially advanced countries (IACs) to characteristics of less developed countries (LDCs).

Step 1	Read the section in your textbook titled *"Comparing Developed and Less-Developed Countries."*
Step 2	Read the Graphing Workshop *"Grasp It!"* exercise titled *"Production Possibilities."* This exercise uses a slider bar to demonstrate economic growth based on the impact of technological change on the production possibilities curve for computers and cars.
Step 3	Create a new graph at the Graphing Workshop *"Try It!"* exercise titled *"Production Possibilities."* This exercise illustrates an outward shift in the production possibilities curve.
Step 4	Play the *"Causation Chains Game"* titled *"Economic Growth."*
Step 5	Listen to the *"Ask the Instructor Video Clip"* titled *"How Important Is the Rate of Economic Growth to You?"* You will learn how much the rate of growth means to the standard of living.
Step 6	Listen to the *"Ask the Instructor Video Clip"* titled *"Why Are Some Nations Rich, But Others Are Poor?"* You will learn the basic factors that determine which nations are rich and poor.
Step 7	Read the *EconDebate* titled *"Is More Spending on Infrastructure the Key to Economic Growth?"* This article describes the importance of infrastructure to economic growth.
The Result	Following these steps, you have learned industrially advanced countries (IACs) are countries in which GDP per capita is high and output is produced by technologically advanced capital. Less-developed countries (LDCs) are countries with low production per person. In these countries, output is produced without large amounts of technologically advanced capital and well-educated labor.

#2 - Understand the role of private investment, the International Monetary Fund (IMF), and World Bank in aiding poor countries.

Step 1   Read the section in your textbook titled *"The Helping Hand of Advanced Countries."*

Step 2   Read the *EconNews* article titled *"Iraq's Economy Slow to Grow."* This article describes the importance of private investment to economic growth.

Step 3   Read the *EconNews* article titled *"Grading the IMF and World Bank."* This article describes the policies and practices of the IMF and World Bank.

Step 4   Read the *EconNews* article titled *"Is Relief the Right Response?"* This article describes arguments concerning debt relief for less-developed countries.

Step 5   Read the *EconDebate* article titled *"Does Foreign Direct Investment Hinder or Help Economic Development?"* This article describes the debate of foreign direct investment.

Step 6   Read the *EconDebate* article titled *"What Are the Pros and Cons of International Monetary Fund (IMF) Involvement with Global Economics?"* This article describes the history of the IMF.

Step 7   Read the *EconDebate* article titled *"Agriculture Key to New Trade Deal."* This article describes the elimination or reduction of subsidies to open new markets in third world countries.

The Result   Following these steps, you have learned the role of private investment, the IMF, and World Bank in helping less-developed countries.

■ COMPLETION QUESTIONS

1. _____ is the value of final goods produced (GDP) divided by the total population.

2. High-income nations which have market economies based on large stocks of technologically advanced capital and well-educated labor are called _____.

3. _____ are nations without large stocks of technologically advanced capital and well-educated labor. LDCs are economies based on agriculture such as most countries of Africa, Asia, and Latin America.

4.   The _____ is a trap in which countries are poor because they cannot afford to save and invest, but they cannot save and invest because they are poor.

5.   Capital goods usually provided by the government, including highways, bridges, waste and water systems, and airports are called _____.

6.   _____ is the transfer of money or resources from one government to another for which no repayment is required.

7.   The agency of the U.S. State Department that is in charge of U.S. aid to foreign countries is called _____.

8.   The _____ is the lending agency that makes long-term low-interest loans and provides technical assistance to less-developed countries.

9.   The _____ is the lending agency that makes short-term conditional low-interest loans to developing countries.

10.   A series of proposals made by LDCs calling for changes that would accelerate the economic growth and development of the LDCs is called _____.

■ MULTIPLE CHOICE

1.   According to the classification in the text, which of the following is *not* an IAC?

   a.   New Zealand.
   b.   Greece.
   c.   United Arab Emirates.
   d.   All of the above are IACs.

2.   The number of countries of the world classified as LDCs is:

   a.   25.
   b.   50.
   c.   75.
   d.   150.
   e.   250.

3.   According to the classification in the text, which of the following is *not* a LDC?

    a.   Hong Kong.
    b.   Israel.
    c.   Argentina.
    d.   Greece.

4.   Which of the following is a problem when comparing GDPs per capita between nations?

    a.   GDP per capita is subject to greater measurements errors for LDCs compared to IACs.
    b.   Fluctuations in exchange rates effect differences in GDP per capita.
    c.   GDP per capita fails to measure income distribution.
    d.   All of the above.
    e.   None of the above.

5.   Which of the following is *not* generally considered to be an ingredient for economic growth?

    a.   Investment in human capital.
    b.   Political instability.
    c.   High savings rate and investment in capital.
    d.   Growth in technology.
    e.   Investment in infrastructure.

6.   Which of the following statements is *true*?

    a.   A less developed country (LDC) is a country with a low GDP per capita, low levels of capital, and uneducated workers.
    b.   The vicious circle of poverty exists because GDP must rise before people can save and invest.
    c.   LDCs are characterized by rapid population growth and low levels of investment in human capital.
    d.   All of the above.

7.   Countries are poor because they cannot afford to save and invest is called the:

    a.   vicious circle of poverty.
    b.   savings-investment trap.
    c.   LDC trap.
    d.   cycle of insufficient credit.

8.   Which of the following is infrastructure?

    a. Police.
    b. Training and education.
    c. Highways.
    d. All of the above.
    e. None of the above.

9.   Which of the following statements is *true*?

    a. There is no single correct strategy for economic growth and development.
    b. In general, GDP per capita is highly correlated with alternative quality of life measures.
    c. The "New International Economic Order" is a set of proposals by LDCs that would give them greater control over the policies of international financial institutions.
    d. All of the above.

10.   Which of the following is true concerning GDP per capita comparisons?

    a. The accuracy of LDC GDP per capita data is questionable.
    b. GDP per capita ignores the degree of income distribution.
    c. GDP per capita is affected by exchange rate changes.
    d. GDP per capita does not account for the difference in the cost of living among nations.
    e. All of the above are true.

11.   International comparisons of per-capita GDP may not reflect standard of living because _____.

    a. Currency exchange rates may not fully account for differences in purchasing power, and thus people in a country with high per-capita GDP may have a lower standard of living because of high local prices for food, housing, or other necessities.
    b. People in some countries enjoy poverty and do not mind a lack of access to medicine, education, nutritious food, and safe drinking water.
    c. Markets do not exist in less-developed countries.
    d. None of the above.

12.   Which of the following *best* describes the cycle of poverty?

    a.   Rich countries eventually decline because is citizens become lazy.

    b.   Poor countries eventually improve through investment in education, infrastructure, and capital accumulation.

    c.   Rich countries stay rich through continued high levels of investment in education, infrastructure, and capital accumulation.

    d.   Poor countries stay poor because they cannot afford to invest in education, infrastructure, and capital accumulation.

13.   Which of the following is an example of a multilateral lending agency that makes loans, rather than gifts of foreign aid, to less-developed countries?

    a.   The Agency for International Development.

    b.   The International Red Cross.

    c.   The World Bank.

    d.   Church World Relief.

14.   Which of the following is *not* a common characteristic of industrially advanced countries (IACs)?

    a.   Market-based economies.

    b.   Large stocks of technologically advanced capital.

    c.   Well-educated labor.

    d.   Low per capita energy consumption.

15.   The poorest regions in the world, as measured by GDP per capita, are:

    a.   Latin America and the Caribbean.

    b.   the Middle East and North Africa.

    c.   Sub-Saharan Africa and South Asia.

    d.   Australia and New Zealand.

16.   GDP per capita is a relatively good measurement of:

    a.   the distribution of income.

    b.   purchasing power.

    c.   household production.

    d.   the standard of living.

17.   Which of the following can be a barrier to an LDC's economic growth and development?

    a.   Low population growth.
    b.   A low level of human capital.
    c.   Faster capital accumulation.
    d.   More infrastructure.

18.   Capital goods provided by the government such as roads, airports, and water systems make up the country's:

    a.   supply of capital.
    b.   infrastructure.
    c.   standard of living.
    d.   political environment.

19.   Which of the following makes short-term, conditional loans to developing countries?

    a.   The Agency for International Development (AID).
    b.   The World Bank.
    c.   The North American Free Trade Agreement (NAFTA).
    d.   The Internation Monetary Fund (IMF).

20.   The "Four Tigers" of East Asia are the newly industrialized countries of Taiwan, South Korea, Hong Kong, and:

    a.   Japan.
    b.   Singapore.
    c.   The Phillippines.
    d.   Vietnam.

■ TRUE OR FALSE

1.   T   F   A country with a high GDP per capita is classified as an IAC.

2.   T   F   According to the text, Singapore is classified as a LDC.

3.   T   F   According to the text, Ireland and Israel are classified as IACs.

4.   T   F   In general, GDP per capita is not highly correlated with alternative measures of quality of life.

5.   T   F   A country can develop without a large natural resource base.

6.   T   F   The vicious circle of poverty is the trap in which the LDC is too poor to save and therefore it cannot invest and remains poor.

7.   T   F   The Agency for International Development is the agency of the U.S. State Department that is in charge of U.S. aid to foreign countries.

■ CROSSWORD PUZZLE

Fill in the crossword puzzle from the list of key concepts. Not all of the concepts are used.

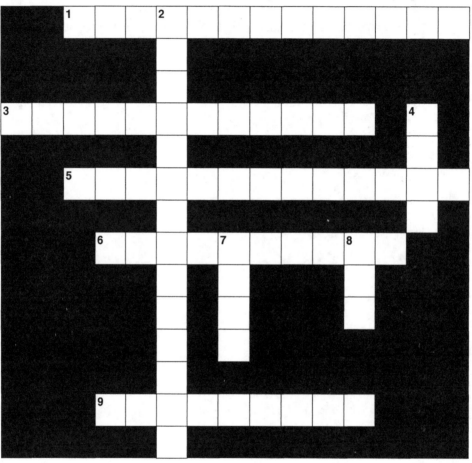

ACROSS

1.   _____ of poverty is the trap in which countries are poor because they cannot afford to save and invest, but they cannot save and invest because they are poor.
3.   The value of final goods produced (GDP) divided by the total population.
5.   _____ countries are nations without large stocks of technologically advanced capital and well-educated labor.
6.   The transfer of money or resources from one government to another for which no repayment is required.
9.   The lending agency that makes long-term low-interest loans and provides technical assistance to less-developed countries.

DOWN

2.   Capital goods usually provided by the government, including highways, bridges, waste and water systems, and airports.
4.   A series of proposals made by LDCs calling for changes that would accelerate the economic growth and development of the LDCs.
7.   High-income nations that have market economies based on large stocks of technologically advanced capital and well-educated labor.
8.   The lending agency that makes short-term conditional low-interest loans to developing countries.

■ ANSWERS

Completion Questions

1. GDP per capita
2. industrially advanced countries (IACs)
3. less-developed countries (LDCs)
4. vicious circle of poverty
5. infrastructure
6. foreign aid
7. Agency for International Development
8. World Bank
9. International Monetary Fund
10. New International Economic Order

Multiple Choice

1. c 2. d 3. a 4. d 5. b 6. d 7. a 8. c 9. d 10. e 11. a 12. d 13. c 14. d 15. c 16. d 17. b 18. b 19. d 20. b

True or False

1. True 2. False 3. True 4. False 5. True 6. True 7. True

Crossword Puzzle